GOING HOME

Sarah was waiting when David parked the car in the hospital driveway. He took the suitcase while a nurse guided Sarah from the wheelchair to the front seat. A bouquet of yellow daisies took the place of a baby in her arms.

Was it only four days since she had kissed Mikey good-bye and left for the hospital? Sarah would allow nothing to mar her homecoming to Mikey. The decision about a placement for the new baby could wait. She desperately needed a few days of normal life. But somehow nothing would be the same—ever again.

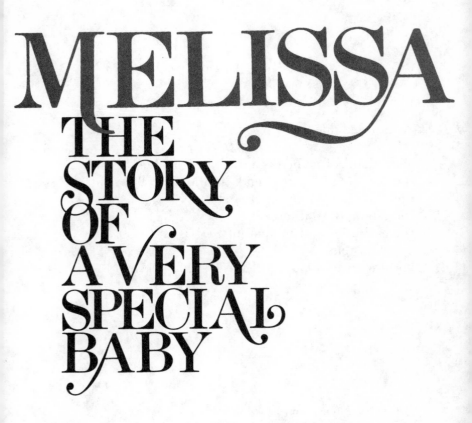

MELISSA
THE STORY OF A VERY SPECIAL BABY

Diane Braunstein Baumgartner

David C. Cook Publishing Co.
ELGIN, ILLINOIS—WESTON, ONTARIO

Acknowledgments

With thanks for the encouragement of Mary Brite,
the prayers of Chris Arends and Milton Whitfield,
the critique of Mary Poore Sell,
the typing of Marge Dohse,
the enthusiasm of my parents, Doris and Bob
   Braunstein,
and the love of God, which is in Christ Jesus.

© 1980 Diane Braunstein Baumgartner

Scripture quotations, except where otherwise noted, are taken from the Revised Standard Version.

Published by David C. Cook Publishing Co.
850 N. Grove Ave., Elgin, IL 60120
Cover design by Graphic Communications, Inc.
Printed in the United States of America

ISBN: 0-89191-233-9
LC: 80-68854

With love and heartfelt appreciation for the ones who made the events of this book possible:
Barbara and Leroy,
my husband, Tony,
and my sons,
Robert,
Shannon,
Chuck, and
Cameron.

For thou didst form my inward parts,
thou didst knit me together in my
    mother's womb. . . .
Thy eyes beheld my unformed
    substance;
in thy book were written, every one
    of them,
the days that were formed for me,
when as yet there was none of them (Psalm 139: 13, 16).

Foreword

Mrs. B.—I think it speaks of Mrs. Baumgartner to know that in a hospital she had come to have just initials. Some of the senior surgeons have not reached that stature.

Her devotion and love to the children that are placed in her care extends far beyond the hospital as she is known and respected by all service agencies who deal with handicapped children.

Successful education is often bidirectional. In this sense, Mrs. Baumgartner has been an educational experience for all of us—staff physicians, residents, interns, nurses, physical therapists—who have managed "her children" with her. We have all had lessons from her in the ability to love and care for our fellow human beings. Her steady faith has often been a support to us when confronted with the loneliness of decision.

The book is not only about Melissa, but is about humanity and Mrs. B.

JACK TREMBATH, M.B., B.S., M.R.C. PSYCH.
Associate Professor of Child Health
The University of Nebraska Medical Center

CONTENTS

Foreword   9
1. "Mommy, I'm All Right"   13
2. "If There Were No One Else to Consider"   23
3. A Very Hurt Baby   29
4. Through Eyes of Love   33
5. A Loan and a Gift   43
6. Lessons with Nancy   53
7. "Search Me, O God"   61
8. Reaching Out   71
9. Home Visit   79
10. A Song in My Heart   87
11. An Answered Prayer   95
12. Miraculously, Our Own   103
Epilogue   109

1

"Mommy, I'm All Right"

Sarah and David had no reason to suspect that the delivery and birth which was about to begin would be anything but routine. Yet deep inside, Sarah felt a persistent uncertainty. As they drove the five miles from their home to the hospital, a drama was unfolding. This birth would change the lives of several people.

Sarah's blonde hair fluttered about her delicate features as an April breeze drifted through the car window. She turned and looked at David. Just watching him seemed to impart security.

"David, don't you think it's odd that Dr. Blake recommended having labor induced?" she asked. "After all, I am still a few days early."

"No. I hear doctors do this all the time. Maybe they don't want to be called out during the night." He reached for her hand and squeezed it.

I guess it's silly to be worried, Sarah decided. She sighed and leaned her head back on the seat.

MELISSA

But the worry remained six hours later in the labor room. While inducing medication dripped slowly from the IV bottle into her arm, Sarah passed the time by watching the continuous graph that clicked out of the fetal monitor beside her bed. The paddles and wires placed on her swollen abdomen fed the monitor information about her contractions and the heartbeat of the baby inside.

Dr. Blake read the graph then examined her again.

"I'm going to break your bag of water, Sarah, to help make the contractions harder," he said, snapping on a pair of rubber surgical gloves.

She looked at the mountain scene that covered the opposite wall and tried to forget her discomfort.

A moment later he had completed the procedure. Sarah thought she detected an expression of surprise on the doctor's face. The excessive amount of amniotic fluid indicated that the fetus may not have been urinating and swallowing properly. But Dr. Blake said nothing to Sarah until much later.

An hour passed before he examined her again. He found that the hard contractions had produced little results. He smiled and tried to reassure her.

"The baby's head just doesn't seem to want to stay pressed against the cervix, but it shouldn't be too much longer. Think you can hang on?" he asked.

Sarah nodded.

Labor continued to progress slowly, almost as if the baby protested leaving the warm, secure world of its mother's womb.

Finally the nurses, now dressed in sterile gowns and masks, wheeled Sarah into the delivery room and helped her onto the draped table. The pink walls were supposed to help expectant mothers relax, but Sarah's anxiety only

14

increased. The sound of forceps slapped into Dr. Blake's hand resounded like the clash of cymbals and anxiety crescendoed into fear.

Horrified, she watched in the overhead mirror as the doctor pulled and tugged at the baby's head.

"What's wrong?" she cried out. "Something must be wrong!" But no one seemed to hear.

"Push, Sarah," was the doctor's only response. "Push hard."

There was only a moment of rest before the onset of the next hard contraction. Cooperating with the bearing down pains, Sarah took a deep breath and strained to push the baby through the birth canal.

At last, the baby's head emerged.

Dr. Blake and the nurse exchanged glances as he reached for the red bulb syringe in her hand. His hands trembled slightly as he suctioned mucus from the baby's nose and mouth.

One final effort and it was over. The baby was born.

"You have a girl," Dr. Blake announced.

Sarah scarcely noticed that he didn't lay the baby across her abdomen while he clamped and cut the umbilical cord, as he had done with her first child, Mikey.

Her eyes followed the doctor as he carried the baby across the room. Carefully he placed her in a small steel bed and switched on the warming lights. A nurse clamped an identification band around the tiny wrist and put drops into the baby's eyes. For several minutes the doctor and nurses hovered over the infant, examining her. Occasionally, one of them turned and looked at Sarah.

But she had forgotten her anxiety. Now she felt only ecstasy. A baby girl! Just what she had hoped for.

After wrapping the newborn in a soft, yellow blanket,

MELISSA

Dr. Blake carried her to Sarah's side. She reached up to take the bundle. But instead of placing the baby in her mother's arms, Dr. Blake held her upright for Sarah to look at. He hesitated, struggling for the right words.

"Sarah, the baby has some problems."

"Problems? What do you mean? What's wrong? She looks all right to me."

"The baby's ears are too low and her head is a little enlarged. There may be some brain damage."

Sarah's joy vanished, replaced by a swirling mass of unreasonable emotions.

"David will be upset with me. The baby will hate me. I'm the one who carried her, so it must be my fault."

"Go ahead and cry," Dr. Blake suggested, awkwardly trying to comfort her.

But tears refused to come.

The nurse's notes recorded the drama that ensued:
10:20 P.M. Noncrying infant carried to intensive-care nursery via arms of Dr. Blake. . . .

Dr. Blake observed as the pediatrician examined the baby. She moved only slightly in response to the pain of a pinprick. The rubber percussion hammer produced almost no response when tapped against her limbs. Their concern mounted.

After carrying the infant into the darkness of the medication room, the pediatrician placed a flashlight against her skull, transilluminating it. The baby's head glowed from each direction in which the light moved. Normally, the thick mass of brain matter would have stopped the passage of light, but cerebrospinal fluid filled most of this baby's enlarged ventricles. Their diagnosis was hydrocephalus (water on the brain).

11 P.M. Temperature 96:2; blood pressure 160/60;

heart rate 112 per minute; color dusky; oxygen started.

Sarah's mother, Jean, stood for a long time at the intensive-care nursery window watching the doctor's examination of the new baby. She had slipped unnoticed from the waiting room to the nursery. But when a nurse saw her she was asked to leave. Hospital policy, she was told.

Jean was angry. Angry that the doctor hadn't waited until someone was with Sarah when she was told the baby had problems. She felt it even more uncaring that neither she nor David was allowed to remain with Sarah through the night.

Around the corner from the nursery, at the far end of the corridor, Sarah lay in the semidarkened recovery room, unable to sleep. The nurse had given her a sedative after David had gone home for the night. Alone now, her sense of isolation seemed magnified. Exhaustion covered her like a heavy blanket. Finally the tears came and she turned her face into the pillow and sobbed. *Why can't I do anything right?* she wondered.

12:30 A.M. Full skull series and chest X-ray done. Cardiac monitor started. Lab work done. IV started via scalp vein. Temperature 96.4. Baby remains inactive.

Sarah dried her eyes at the sound of footsteps. It was Dr. Blake followed by the pediatrician.

"Dr. Blake promised to let you know what we found after examining the baby," the pediatrician said. "She has *hydrocephalus;* it means fluid on the brain. That's why her head is enlarged. Later, if it appears to be growing too fast, we may need to insert a shunt, which acts like a pump and diverts the excess fluid from the head into the abdominal cavity.

"We will need to consult a neurosurgeon and a couple of other specialists. After they have examined the baby and we have some test results, we'll be able to tell you more—perhaps tomorrow."

Tomorrow would be soon enough. David and Dr. Michaels, the family physician, would be with her then. Sarah knew her doctor would explain the things she couldn't understand and answer the questions racing through her mind.

6 A.M. Heart rate 175 per minute; occasional weak cry; cloudiness in right eye has increased. Blank stare noted. Infant remains lethargic. Head and right arm continue to be bruised.

7 A.M. Temperature 103.2; isolette 98 degrees; isolette opened. Cool sponging done to infant.

8 A.M. Temperature 99.4; infant repositioned frequently. Water mattress inserted under head. Continues to be inactive.

11 A.M. Father viewing through window.

Sarah tried to be brave when David came into her room. His eyes were red and swollen and she suspected he hadn't slept much either. David made no attempt at useless words of reassurance. It wasn't necessary. His presence was what Sarah needed most. Just being held in his arms assured her no problem was insurmountable.

Specialists came and went throughout the day: a neurosurgeon, an opthalmologist, a geneticist, the pediatrician, and Dr. Blake—each making vague comments. They seemed to be uncomfortable and hurried out of the room as if they didn't want to be questioned.

Sarah felt as if even the nurses were avoiding her.

12:30 P.M. Number six french tube passed through nose for gavage feeding of nonsucking infant. Temperature, low; wrapped in blanket.
4 P.M. Fifteen cc formula given through gavage tube; IV still in place; infusing well. Temperature 97.4; color pale; blank facial expression.

A nurse removed the untouched supper tray from the room as Dr. Michaels pulled the privacy curtain around Sarah's corner of the four-bed ward. The elderly doctor had been her physician since she was a child. Although he spoke with fatherly concern for Sarah and David, he was brutally honest about the baby's condition.

"We don't know if the baby will live more than a few months. At the present time she's not sucking and may never learn how. If she lives, she'll always require an enormous amount of care. She will certainly never crawl or walk or feed herself. We suspect she is blind and possibly has a hearing impairment. In any case, she'll never know you."

There was nothing left; not the tiniest thread of hope. Only the stabbing knife of guilt remained. Dr. Michaels assured Sarah that even unknowingly she couldn't have caused this to happen. He explained that the birth defects began four to six weeks after conception, before Sarah even knew she was pregnant. But nothing he said removed the overwhelming guilt she felt.

As Dr. Michaels's voice droned on Sarah only half heard that caring for a severely handicapped child could put great stress on a marriage. Divorce statistics for parents of terminally ill children were equally high.

"It is the consensus of the physicians that I recommend

you do not take this baby home. Of course, the two of you will have to decide what you can accept for yourselves, morally. But I suggest you place her in a home. Try to find a placement that will not administer life-support treatment if the baby should begin to fail. We're unable to do that here. As long as the baby remains hospitalized we must do everything possible to keep her alive."

Twenty-four hours ago Sarah and David had a baby to hope and plan and dream for. Now their dreams were gone and there was no hope. Perhaps it would be better if the baby died; better for the baby. Better for everyone.

Two days passed and except for that first brief moment in the delivery room, Sarah had not seen the baby. She had been unable to face any thoughts of going to the nursery window. Perhaps she could have if there had been no one watching. But she was afraid—afraid of what she'd find, afraid of falling to pieces. David seemed to share her fears and had discouraged her from seeing the baby.

Sarah woke early on the third morning just as dawn broke into a pink sky. New desire made her determined that today she would see her baby.

She needed someone to be with her when she went to the nursery window and her mother seemed to be the natural choice. Sarah knew she could count on Jean's strength and stability.

Awaiting her mother's arrival, Sarah went to the empty waiting room at the end of the hall. She often escaped to this room and drank a glass of juice while the other mothers had their babies at feeding time.

For a long while she stood at the window, looking down into the cemetery one-half block away, unable to free herself from the slow-motion world of depression. Sarah thought it ironic that the distance from the hospital to the cemetery was so short.

What is life all about, anyway? she asked herself. You are born, you live, then die. What is the purpose of it all? There must be more. There *has* to be more. I am only going through the motions of living. Nothing seemed real to her right now.

Perhaps she could force herself to be happy again, to think positively: *It's a warm spring day. The flowers in the cemetery are lovely.* But the words seemed empty and again tears trickled down her cheeks.

"Sarah," the nurse interrupted, "your mother is here."

For a long moment the two women embraced. Then linking their arms together they walked slowly out of the waiting room and down the hall, past the healthy newborns' nursery, to the intensive-care window.

"Mother, please don't say anything. Just hold onto my arm."

Sarah hesitated for just a moment longer and surveyed the other babies farther back in the room. They were tiny premature infants with respirator hoses taped across their mouths. It was a frightening scene, yet Sarah knew most of those babies were better off than hers.

Finally she lowered her eyes to the isolette in front of her.

The baby seemed to turn her head toward Sarah. She opened her eyes and looked up. Sarah gasped. Was the baby *looking* at her? It seemed as if she were. That expression on her face! Sarah sensed, somehow, the baby was trying to say, "Mommy, I'm all right. It's not your fault."

Sarah's hand covered her mouth, as she tried to muffle the sounds of her own sobbing. She felt her mother grip even more tightly on her arm.

Can the baby see me? Sarah wondered. They said she is

blind. But she seems to be looking at me. Maybe she isn't so bad. Maybe the doctors are wrong. Maybe the baby will be all right after all.

Then as swiftly as it had come, hope was gone again. There were tears in Sarah's eyes as she turned from the nursery window. Perhaps they would always be there.

The next day Sarah was released from the hospital. She was waiting when David parked the car in the hospital driveway. He took the suitcases while the nurse guided Sarah from the wheelchair into the front seat. A bouquet of yellow daisies took the place of a baby in her arms.

Was it only four days ago that she had kissed Mikey good-bye and left for the hospital? She couldn't wait to squeeze her son and feel his chubby arms around her neck.

David had already told Mikey that mommy would not be bringing home a baby. The three year old listened nonchalantly, then ran back to the swing in the backyard.

Sarah would allow nothing to mar her homecoming to Mikey. The decision about a placement for the new baby would wait. She desperately needed a few days of normal life. But somehow nothing would be quite the same ever again.

2

"If There Were No One Else to Consider"

A few days later Sarah crossed the living room in answer to the telephone's insistent ring. She glanced briefly at the yellow bassinet, now a casket that held dead hopes and dreams. Sarah had left the bassinet just as it was, a constant reminder to accept reality.

"Sarah. My name is Ann. I am a social worker for the Human Service Agency. The hospital has made a referral to our agency indicating that you may be needing a placement for your baby daughter."

"Yes. That's right."

"I'd like to meet with both you and your husband. When would it be convenient for me to talk with you?"

After agreeing that Ann could come to the house the following Tuesday, Sarah slowly replaced the receiver. She was relieved that something was going to be done, yet annoyed with David. Hadn't he promised that he would take care of arrangements for the baby's placement? And what about his decision to talk with their priest, to be certain that they were moving in a direction that was morally right? For that matter, what had happened to the closeness they had always shared?

The subtle changes occurring in their marriage couldn't be seen by friends. But privately the tension was obvious. Oh, she and David still talked—about everything except the baby. Was it only because they were afraid of hurting each other that they couldn't discuss what had happened? Sarah wasn't certain of anything anymore.

She didn't understand why she had become so talkative lately and was astonished to find herself engaged in long conversations with virtual strangers about nothing in particular. Neither did she understand why David seemed unable to talk to anyone and grew more quiet, almost withdrawn, as the days passed.

On one occasion when she had approached David about her desire to visit the baby, she was jolted by his furious reply. "No. That's not a good idea. Forget it!"

"But, David, I'm not going to ask to bring her home, if that's what you're afraid of. I just want to see her, that's all."

"You know what the doctor said. She . . . she'll never even know you." The door slammed loudly behind him as he left the house.

Frustration exploded into anger as Sarah shouted at the closed door. "What is *wrong* with you, David? Sometimes I wonder if you feel anything at all!"

Sarah found it incredible that now, when she needed David most, he had shut himself away from her. At times, she wondered if their marriage was going to end up as empty as the yellow bassinet.

When the nurse called and asked that they come to the hospital to view the results of Melissa's brain scan, Sarah was hesitant to mention it to David. But she knew they must face the results of this test. The nurse had also explained that they would have to sign permission forms for shunt surgery to release some of the water on Melissa's brain.

She mentioned the call at dinner that evening, but David said nothing to indicate that he realized how important this test was, only a quick, "OK, I'll leave work a little early tomorrow afternoon." Even now as they drove toward the hospital Sarah knew he was pretending to be absorbed in the afternoon traffic to avoid talking about the ordeal that lay ahead.

It was almost five when Sarah and David entered the hospital. Watching the gray marble floor disappear under her footsteps, Sarah momentarily imagined herself and David to be death-row prisoners, hoping beyond hope for a last-minute reprieve from certain execution.

She allowed herself one last fantasy: the doctors had made a terrible mistake and the baby only had some type of tumor that could be removed by surgery, making her all right. But once in the neurosurgeon's office her fantasy was no match for the reality of the brain scan.

"An EMI scan is similar to a series of X-ray pictures," the doctor explained. "The revolving scanner takes multiple views and electronically puts them together, giving us a two-dimensional look inside."

He pointed to one of the smaller pictures on a large sheet that had been clipped to a lighted screen. "I believe this top view of the baby's head will give you the best understanding of our findings. This white circle, here, indicates the shape of the skull."

"But I don't see anything inside the circle!" Sarah

exclaimed. "There is only blackness."

"Mostly, yes, with the exception of the small amount of light gray area around the perimeter of the skull. That indicates there are just a few centimeters of cerebral cortex."

David's face was ashen.

"But how can she even be alive with so little brain matter?" Sarah questioned. "How is it possible for anyone to live with almost no brain?"

"The brain stem appears to be intact. It is one of the most important parts of the brain since all the involuntary functions are controlled there: sucking, heart rate, respiration, and so forth. With so much of the higher part of the brain missing, a meaningful life is simply not possible for this child."

Sarah was stunned by the clinical, factual manner in which the doctor had presented his information. He seemed unaware that he was speaking of a person, *their* baby.

Maybe she wouldn't have a meaningful life and would only live for a few months, but she was still their child. Wasn't it their responsibility to take her home and do what they could? The neurosurgeon seemed to read her thoughts.

"Perhaps you have considered taking the baby home and allowing her to die there. Frankly, I would advise against it. I believe that when the time came, you would find yourselves unable to stand by and do nothing. It may be difficult to find a placement that will. Have you checked into a possible home for her yet?"

David shook his head. "No. We do have an appointment with a social worker from the Human Service Agency in a few days."

"Well, it's possible that they can help you. Some of

these agency people are very well meaning—good people, you understand—but they tend to be very positive, very hopeful. I hope you won't get caught up in all of that. Investing time and money and energy in a child like this is rather useless. The state institution for the mentally retarded is probably your best alternative."

David nodded slowly. "We understand. How long before she is discharged?"

"You still have a couple of weeks to make arrangements. As the nurse explained on the telephone, the baby's head is enlarging and we have scheduled her for shunt surgery tomorrow. As soon as her condition has stabilized again, she will be released. The forms you need to sign are in the nursery. Stop up there on your way out."

Out in the hallway, a shiver of fear ran through Sarah as they waited for the elevator. How she wished the forms could have been signed in the doctor's office!

She was still trembling when the nurse led them through the doors of the intensive-care nursery to within a few feet of the baby. *Why are they forcing us to come into this room and stand right next to her?* Sarah wondered. She tucked her hands inside of her folded arms to hide their shaking.

What is wrong with me anyway? she questioned. *For days I have wanted to come and see her. Now I am so frightened I don't want to look at her.*

Finally, for the nurse's sake, Sarah turned toward her baby and smiled. She supposed that's what was expected of her: smile, be happy, be brave.

"Would you like me to open the porthole so you could touch your baby?" the nurse asked.

"Oh, no! I couldn't touch her! I mean, I'd be too frightened," Sarah stammered. But she was unable to prevent her eyes from caressing the infant. With her eyes she touched the baby's tiny feet, stroked her thin body, and brushed the soft skin of her cheek.

Inside, the thing she feared most began to happen, she had a wild urge to tell the baby, *Oh, honey! Mommy just wishes she could reach in, grab you up in her arms, and run away with you.*

She fought back the tears and only a slight, hysterical giggle escaped her lips. *Wouldn't that be funny? Mommy kidnapping you and running away. Isn't that ridiculous? Where would I hide with a naked baby? But if only there was no one else to consider, I would . . . I would!*

David touched her arm and indicated that they should move on. Sarah wondered what he had been thinking as they stood looking at their baby.

It was dark when David and Sarah reached home. David pulled the car into the driveway and turned off the ignition. Quietly he reached for Sarah and drew her head to his shoulder. His gentle kiss on her forehead and soft caress of her hair said the words for him. Sarah felt tears trickle down David's cheek and mingle with her own.

3

A Very Hurt Baby

David took the Tuesday evening paper and reclined in his favorite brown chair while Sarah cleared the supper dishes from the table and Mikey ran outside to play. It was nearly seven when the doorbell rang. Sarah glanced out the window and dried her hands on a towel.

"David. It's the social worker from the Human Service Agency," she called.

Opening the door, she was greeted by petite, brown-eyed Ann. Instantly, Sarah judged that she and Ann were about the same age. But there was one painful difference. Ann was pregnant. Very pregnant. It seemed like a cruel joke. *Why?* Sarah questioned. *Of all the social workers I could have gotten, why does it have to be someone who is pregnant?*

Uncertain if she should laugh, or cry, or be angry, Sarah escorted Ann into the living room and introduced her to David. He answered her routine questions: dates of birth, number of children, place of employment.

MELISSA

Sarah drifted in and out of their conversation, only half listening.

She told herself it was foolish to be upset and ridiculous to be jealous of Ann. But still she felt resentful of every pregnant woman's happiness.

Ann finished the questions and closed her briefcase.

"How could our agency help you at this time?" she asked. "If we can provide you with a staff person to come part of each day, would you like to try to bring the baby home?"

Sarah interrupted her longing gaze at Ann's swollen stomach. "No," she answered, wondering if Ann would understand, if anyone would understand. It wasn't that she didn't want to bring the baby home. She couldn't.

"Perhaps you would be interested in meeting with our pilot parents group," Ann offered. "Families who have been through these things with their own children meet once a month to share problems and solutions. One of the more experienced parents pilots, or helps, one of the newer families."

To Sarah's relief, David repeated her answer. "No, we have decided to accept the recommendation made by the doctors to place her in the state institution."

Ann hesitated. It was never easy to inform parents that they didn't always have the only voice in the placement of their child.

"I'm sorry. I guess no one has explained. Because of a legal suit brought by several parents of mentally retarded children in this area, the court has ruled that it is the right of every child to live in the least restrictive environment, regardless of his handicaps. When an appropriate placement can be found for the child within the local community, the child must remain within his community."

"You mean we *can't* send her to the institution?" David was incredulous. "But we can't afford the expense of private care. We would be in debt for years if the baby lives longer than anyone expects."

"The cost of a placement with our agency is the same as the charges for institutionalization," Ann assured him. "Both are based on the same small percentage of your monthly income."

When neither Sarah or David spoke, Ann continued.

"Perhaps I could suggest this. Our agency has a residence at the County Hospital for medically fragile, mentally retarded children. When the baby is discharged from the hospital, we could place her there for two or three months. At the end of that time we could again discuss the possibility of your bringing her home.

"If you still felt you would be unable to care for her, I would recommend placing Melissa with a home teacher in an alternative living unit. The arrangement is similar to a foster home, only our home teachers are agency staff persons trained to care for the severely handicapped and mentally retarded. Would that be agreeable to you?"

Sarah and David looked at each other and nodded. "Fine," Sarah replied. "I find it difficult to believe that anyone will want to take her as a foster child, but we won't be bringing her home."

Ann obtained Sarah's and David's signatures on several release forms. She said she would contact them again after seeing the baby and making arrangements for her placement at the children's residence.

Driving home after her visit to the parents, Ann saw the lighted windows of the hospital in the distance and made an impulsive decision to stop and visit the baby.

At the nursery scrub sink, she lathered her hands with the brown antiseptic and slipped into a sterile gown. An intern stepped briskly past her and pointed to her bulging stomach under the gown.

"Lady, aren't you in the wrong department? Labor and Delivery are down the hall," he said. They both laughed.

But Ann was beginning to feel a bit queasy. It was the same sensation she always had before seeing one of the new babies on her case load. After reading the list of handicaps and birth defects, she could never be certain what awaited her. What if the baby was a terribly deformed creature? Even though she was a social worker and was expected to handle these things, Ann was uncertain what her response would be.

Taking a deep breath, she stepped into the nursery. A nurse directed her to the isolette and her new client. Ann looked inside and sighed with relief. She was just a baby, a very hurt baby. Flowered paper letters taped on the back of the isolette spelled M-E-L-I-S-S-A.

"Hello, little Melissa," Ann said, tapping her finger on the porthole. "You and I are going to be friends. I'll be back to visit you again soon."

4

Through Eyes of Love

If I had believed in chance, perhaps I would have said it was coincidence that Ann and I met in the parking lot of the supermarket that warm, May afternoon. But I no longer believed in happenstance. I knew God had a plan for my life. There were occasions, however, when I was reluctant to fit into that plan. This was to be one of those times.

Ann had been the social worker for many of the foster children who had been in our home over the past five years. While the carryout boy filled the back of my station wagon with bags of groceries, Ann and I chatted. She had updated me on the progress of several of our former foster children when suddenly her face lit up and I could sense a request was coming even before she voiced it.

"Say, speaking of foster children, Diane, I have a new client. A baby girl."

"Sorry, not me," I protested. "Cameron, my youngest,

is eleven years old. Who needs diapers and nighttime feedings again?"

Ann ignored my comment and continued. "She's five weeks old, and her name is Melissa. She will be discharged from the hospital soon and I will be moving her to the Developmental Maximation Unit (DMU) at County Hospital. Why don't you visit her there?"

I intended to refuse but (perhaps because social workers have a way of looking terribly disappointed) I reluctantly agreed to make one visit to the baby.

"Fantastic," Ann enthused. "Phone me after you've seen her and we'll talk further." She waved and scurried off.

"Now, Ann, wait a second," I called. "I only agreed to *visit*. That's all!"

Somehow I had the strange feeling that I had said yes to more than I knew.

It was almost suppertime that evening when I heard the kitchen door close and a moment later felt the soft brush of my husband's moustache against my cheek.

"Mmm. What's for supper? Smells delicious," Tony said. He gave me a big hug and kiss just as Cameron bounded into the room from baseball practice.

"Oh, no! Mushy stuff," the eleven year old exclaimed, pulling his baseball cap lower over his eyes. I had almost forgotten what Cameron's forehead looked like since the baseball cap had become a permanent fixture on his head. He even slept in the hat, with a baseball glove and ball curled up in one arm.

Cameron relayed the sad news that his team had lost their practice game. I gave him a reassuring hug and sent him to wash for supper.

Tony poured a glass of iced tea and unfolded the evening paper.

"What's new today, honey?" he asked.

"Just the usual: laundry, cleaning, grocery shopping. Oh, by the way, I met Ann at the supermarket. She mentioned a new client she'd like me to visit, a baby girl."

Tony lowered the paper and peered over the top of it. "Diane, you aren't considering taking a *baby*, are you? After all the times I've heard you say . . ."

"Of course not," I interrupted. "No babies for me. That's what I told Ann. But, well, I did sort of agree to visit her once," I added sheepishly.

Tony grinned and nodded his head in mock belief. I laughed, remembering the many times I had seen that same look in the past five years, following our decision to foster parent a special-needs child. Even from the first it was difficult to say no to a social worker's request for a child in need of a home. Our foster parenting experiences, therefore, began with not one child as intended, but two—Doug and Lori.

Doug was a small ten-year-old child with Down's syndrome and a ravenous appetite for food, especially if it was drowned in catsup. The menu mattered little to Doug as long as he had a bottle of catsup to douse on everything.

If Doug's appetite for food was insatiable, so was his enthusiasm for life itself. He was equally content playing in the little league, singing in church, or washing supper dishes. His kind of happiness was contagious, infecting everyone.

Doug had spent several years in the state institution for the mentally retarded. After returning to the community, he lived for a time in a children's hostel with five other retarded youth. Perhaps that's why it seemed to be so special to Doug to just be a "regular kid" with a "regular family."

MELISSA

The fears we'd had about Doug's being accepted by neighborhood children were unfounded. He was received as an equal, which meant he could be fought with as well as played with (apparently the ultimate privilege among little boys).

It was shortly after Doug began to spend weekends with our family in preparation for moving day that Tony and I were asked to consider taking a child in a wheelchair. We had good reason to be hesitant. Seven-year-old Lori was not only mentally retarded but multihandicapped as well. We were told her birth defects included *hydrocephalus* and *spina bifida* (an open spine which left her paralyzed below mid-chest). She also had a ureterostomy, an opening on her side through which urine flowed into a specially fitted bag.

I had been a nurse's aide for several years and knew Lori would require a great deal of care, physically and medically. I was doubtful we were ready to make that kind of commitment. Besides, it was already apparent that Doug would fit well into our household of four sons. Nevertheless, Tony and I consented to visit the crisis unit where Lori was awaiting placement.

Located in the university area of the city, the three-story, red brick crisis home had a quiet elegance about it. Tony and I paused in the doorway of the family room and glanced at one another, then at the little girl waiting by the fireplace.

Lori looked every bit like a Christmas package when we saw her in her apple red dress.

Before long, Tony coaxed her out of the wheelchair into his lap. Tilting her head to one side, she studied Tony's face.

"Are you my friend?" she asked timidly.

Tony assured her that indeed he was. She pondered

his response for a long while, then snuggled against his neck and whispered into his ear.

"You might take me home . . . might you?"

That clinched it! Tony was hooked. We would be taking *two* foster children.

A few days later, we took the boys to the crisis home to meet Lori. They were just as enchanted with her as Tony and I. They were equally enthusiastic about having a wheelchair in the family. Being Lori's brothers would give them the special privilege of operating it, both with and without Lori in it.

One afternoon, after Lori had been with us about six months, Rob, our oldest son, sat at the kitchen table rubbing his knees, obviously in pain from a recent football injury. Playing on the floor across the room, Lori observed his discomfort and with tremendous effort pulled herself by the forearms—her paralyzed legs flopping uselessly behind—until she lay under the table at Rob's feet. Reaching up, she placed her hand gently on his husky leg.

"You might let me pray for you . . . might you, Rob?" she asked sweetly.

He nodded. "Sure, Lori."

Squeezing her eyes tightly closed, she prayed simply. "Jesus, please heal Rob's legs and don't let 'em hurt no more. Amen!"

Tears stung my eyes and a lump formed in my throat at the paradox of a crippled child, one who would never walk and could feel no pain in her own legs, praying for the healing of healthy legs like Rob's. I would never forget her childlike faith in God.

But Lori not only prayed for others (including Bootsie, the family cat), she also told everyone she met about her friend Jesus. One day as we rode in the backseat of a taxi cab, I locked the knees on Lori's braces enabling her to stand and look over the front seat. For a few blocks we rode in silence, then Lori tapped the elderly taxi driver on the shoulder and asked, "Did ya know Jesus lives in my heart?"

Stunned by the question, the man was momentarily speechless. "You . . . ah, you don't say?" he replied.

"Yup." Lori affirmed. "And, he can live in your heart, too."

"How's that?" the driver asked, adjusting the rearview mirror until Lori's reflection appeared.

"Well, it's like this. When Jesus knocks on the door of your heart, you just say, 'Come in' and he will!"

"Is that so?"

"Sure, He died on the cross for you, too, ya know," Lori concluded just as we arrived at our destination.

The Bible says, "A little child shall lead them" (Isa. 11: 6). In so many ways Doug and Lori led and taught us. From them we learned that although the mind and body are damaged, it is the spirit that responds to the truth of God's Word and to his love. Spiritual truth is not dependent on the ability to humanly comprehend.

Doug's and Lori's return to their natural families was a time we had prayed for and yet dreaded. Loving someone you can't keep forever is the bittersweet part of foster parenting, a part that leaves gaping holes in one's heart.

In the months and years that followed Doug's and Lori's leaving, the empty space in our home was filled by forty other foster children. As our confidence grew and our skills increased, we said yes to even the profoundly retarded; children who could not walk or talk or feed themselves. Some had epileptic seizures or cerebral palsy; others were deaf or blind. But most of all, they were unique individuals, children to whom we could be an expression of God's love.

Tony and I wondered how our own sons would respond to having these severely handicapped children in our home, their home as well. Would they resent the sacrifice and sharing required of them? Or would these special foster children be a means of building into all of us the character of Christ?

The boys themselves provided the answer:

"I think Mike really likes it here, don't you? He smiles at me all the time and when he first came he wouldn't smile at all."

"I don't see why everyone doesn't take retarded kids. There's really nothing wrong with them."

As the boys developed a pride in the small accomplishments of our foster children, they lost all concept of the meaning of *retarded*. To them, everyone was smart in his own way.

Mike, our most recent foster child, left to join his parents a few days after my meeting with Ann in the parking lot. School had been dismissed for the summer and the house was silent. Rob and Shannon had dashed off for the first day of swimming and Cameron headed for baseball practice. Only Chuck remained at home, sitting quietly at the dining-room table, gluing together a model sports car.

"Chuck, how about you and me going for an ice-cream cone?" I suggested.

"Sounds great, mom."

"Afterward, I thought we might stop at DMU and visit a baby that Ann told me about."

"Sure. It's OK with me."

Chuck, our third son, was quiet and easygoing by nature, content to tinker for hours with mechanical and electrical things. He seemed to keep his private thoughts and questions tucked away for times like this, when we were alone. I knew we would share more than an ice-cream cone and a short drive in the car before the day was over.

We reached County Hospital at midafternoon. I stopped at the nurses' station for directions.

"Melissa is in the sunroom," the nurse said, pointing the way. "Go right on in."

From a distance, I could already see the infant snuggled into a miniature beanbag chair in the center of the room. As we approached, I noted her pale color and thin body.

"Oh, mom!" Chuck exclaimed. "Isn't she sweet? She sort of looks like a Martian baby. I mean, her head is big and her eyes stick out a little."

I smiled at Chuck's candor. There was no ridicule in his words. He was simply stating facts. It was obvious from the expression on his face that those facts made Melissa more endearing to him.

"Chuck, remember Lori had hydrocephalus, too. I'll bet as Melissa grows and fills out her body will catch up to her head size and she won't look much different than other babies."

"Mom, think we could hold her?"

Was this my shy, reserved, thirteen-year-old son, asking to hold a baby? Trying to conceal my surprise at Chuck's request, I instructed him to sit Indian style on the floor and placed a small blanket over his arm. Carefully sliding one hand behind Melissa's head and another under her bottom, I lifted her from the beanbag chair.

The lifelessness of her body stunned me. She felt different than any baby I had ever held. Her head was heavier than anticipated and her arms and legs dangled as if she were a rag doll.

For several moments Chuck held Melissa in his arms, silently examining her. When he spoke, his voice was almost inaudible.

"Mom, do you think we could keep her?"

"Well . . . I . . . we just came to visit, son." I stammered. "Remember?" Why did those words sound villainous, even to me? I really didn't want to take a baby, did I? We had never taken babies before. Our foster children had always been school age.

But looking at the helpless infant in my son's arms caused every mothering instinct I had ever felt begin to rumble inside me, threatening at any moment to become a small earthquake.

Perhaps it wasn't just that babies required so much time and care that we had only taken school-age children. Maybe I was afraid of becoming more attached than I wanted to be, of caring more than I wanted to care. Maybe there was no longer room in my heart for holes left by departing foster children.

5

A Loan and a Gift

"Hey, dad! Guess what?" Chuck said excitedly as Tony came in the door.

"Mom and I went to see that little baby today, you know, Melissa? She's really neat, dad. Her fingers and toes are so tiny. It's just that her head is sort of big. But she doesn't look *bad* or anything like that, does she, mom?" he asked, turning to me.

I shook my head and made a hasty exit to the kitchen to escape Tony's raised eyebrows and the familiar I-told-you-so smile.

"Want to go with us to see her tonight, dad?"

"Oh? Are you going for a *second* visit?" Tony questioned in mock surprise. He raised his voice to be certain every word reached me in the kitchen.

"So you and mom are going to see the baby again, huh, Chuck?" Tony peeked his head around the corner to get the full benefit of his teasing. To his delight, I had covered my face with a dish towel to conceal my laughter.

MELISSA

"All right, you win," I conceded. "Now, will you come with us to see Melissa?"

Tony agreed and by the time we had finished supper, Chuck's intriguing description of the baby had coaxed the rest of the boys into joining us.

The atmosphere of the DMU at County Hospital seemed more like a children's dormitory than a hospital ward. Royal blue carpet flowed down the halls into the bedrooms and sunroom. Along the walls wooden animals marched: a yellow giraffe, a polka-dot hippo, a toothless tiger, and a smiling, green frog. Even the nurses' attire was casual; uniforms were not worn here. Only the row of positioning wheelchairs and adaptive equipment gave evidence of the special-needs children who lived in the unit.

Beanbag chairs now dotted the floor of the sunroom, giving the school-age children relief from the rigid positioning of their wheelchairs. Melissa's tiny white beanbag was empty. We found her in the dining area being fed a bottle of formula by a male nurse.

Tony carried her to the soft, brown couch in the sunroom and our boys huddled around for a better look at the infant. Tony's affection was immediate. I saw the look in his eyes; the same I had seen on Chuck's face when he had held Melissa.

"Diane, she's precious! Look at her little face. She's beautiful, isn't she, boys?"

Beautiful? Is it possible to perceive beauty in such a terribly handicapped baby? I wondered. Yes, it is possible when God gives the ability to see others as he does—through eyes of love. God sees each of his children not only as they *are* but also as they are *becoming*. I knew Tony

44

was seeing Melissa just that way.

While the boys took turns holding Melissa, Tony and I went around the room and spoke to each of the other children. None were able to talk, but some vocalized sounds in response to our greeting. Others managed a smile when tickled or hugged.

Three-month-old Katey, the only other infant at the unit, was napping in a swinging cradle. She seemed doll-like in a miniature calico dress. Because of a severe heart defect, her skin had a bluish cast to it even as she slept. A thin feeding tube had been taped across her nose since even the effort of sucking caused extreme exertion.

After we said good night to Melissa, Tony nestled her back into the beanbag chair and tucked a soft blanket around her. Restless now, the boys raced each other down the elevators and out to the car while Tony and I stopped at the nurses' station.

Two women and a small boy passed behind us. I watched as they went toward Melissa. The younger woman knelt, hesitantly touching the baby's face. Tears rolled down her cheeks. A nurse confirmed their identities: Melissa's mother, brother, and grandmother.

Long-forgotten memories surfaced within me of Lori and her mother, Joan. After returning Lori from a weekend visit, Joan had cried. Lori had cried. Then I had cried. The parents of our foster children were often facing the most stressful times in their lives. They hurt, cared, suffered, and wept. It was obvious that Melissa's family was grieving, their wounds still fresh and painful. Would the simple hello Tony and I said as we left convey the unspoken message that said we cared?

In the days that followed, the baby at County Hospital

was scarcely out of my thoughts even though the house bustled with the summer activities of four boys. I was content, for a time, to phone the nurses' station and inquire about her. Before long, however, I found excuses to drive by the hospital and drop in for visits.

Most often on those quiet, early summer afternoons, Melissa slept while I held and rocked her. Occasionally, I arrived at feeding time and encouraged her weak attempts at sucking a bottle. The instinct was still poorly developed and a high, narrow palate made sucking even more difficult. Some days she managed to finish two ounces of formula within an hour. On other days, even if the feeding was long overdue, she tired quickly and drifted off to sleep.

The days passed quickly and gradually I began to feel less awkward handling her limp body. And as my confidence in feeding her grew, I considered bringing Melissa home for an afternoon. After all, I reasoned, the care she was receiving at the unit could certainly be managed at home for a few hours. I knew how thrilled Tony and the boys would be to have her all to themselves for a while.

We set the date for July fourth. Gary, the nursing supervisor, secured the necessary release from the physician and Melissa's parents were notified of the time she would be out of the unit. The weatherman forecasted summer showers. But Tony and the boys easily traded a leisurely afternoon at home with Melissa for canceled picnic plans.

Waking early the morning of the fourth, I scurried around after breakfast, preparing fried chicken, baked beans, and potato salad. Anticipation electrified the air. It was eleven o'clock when I phoned the hospital to say I would be arriving soon.

"Diane, I'm sorry. I should have called. Melissa isn't

doing very well," the nurse informed me. "Dr. Rice is with her now. We've notified her parents that she may not make it."

"May not make it?" I repeated. How could she become so ill so quickly? Everything seemed to be fine only yesterday. The gray, cloudy skies now seemed to reflect the heaviness I felt inside. I mumbled "Thank you" and hung up the telephone. That afternoon, looking out the window at the pouring rain, I rethought the hours spent with Melissa, almost regretting becoming involved with her. I knew it was too late for that now. I was already more emotionally attached to her than I had ever wanted to be.

It was late evening when the rain stopped. I slipped on a sweater and drove to the hospital. But even at Melissa's crib side I felt helpless. She was pale and unresponsive. The clear green oxygen mask almost enveloped her tiny face. There would be no holding and rocking her today. I washed her face with a soft, warm cloth and moistened her dry lips with a lemon-glycerine swab. Useless gestures? Perhaps, but it comforted me to be doing something for her.

"How is Melissa, honey?" Tony asked when I returned home. "Is she all right?" His teasing about my visits with Melissa had stopped long ago and his concern for her equaled my own.

"It's pneumonia. Her temperature has dropped below normal and she isn't putting up much of a fight."

The best thing we could do was pray.

Each change of shift I telephoned the nurses' station until Melissa stabilized. Her condition improved rapidly and by the end of the week she was well again and permitted out of her crib. My afternoon visits resumed.

A new date was arranged for the home visit. When that

day arrived, it was Cameron's coveted privilege to ac-
company me to the hospital and hold Melissa as we drove
home. Needing to make a brief stop at the neighborhood
bakery, I asked Cameron if he'd prefer to wait in the car
with Melissa.

"I'll only be a moment," I assured him.

"Mom, couldn't we take Melissa inside?" he asked. "I
know those people would like to see her, too." He was
fairly bursting with pride in his role of big brother. I
hoped he wouldn't be too disappointed if others didn't
see handicapped babies quite the way he did.

Cameron pushed the cart with Melissa sleeping inside
while I shopped. The wide grin from under his baseball
cap was irrestible to everyone. If the clerks and customers
noted that Melissa looked different than other babies,
they gave no indication to Cameron.

"How old is the baby?" one lady asked. "She must be
very sweet."

"What is your new baby sister's name?" another asked.
"Melissa? Well, that's a very pretty name." Cameron gave
no hint that she wasn't exactly *our* baby.

"*See,* mom," he said triumphantly when we returned to
the car. "I told you they'd want to see her."

"Yup, Cam', I guess you were right," I answered,
ruffling his hair. "Everyone must love babies."

That afternoon visit with Melissa at home was just the
first of many. It was delightful caring for a baby again.
The visits went smoothly and I was soon asking myself if
it wasn't silly to be driving to and from the hospital so
frequently? Why didn't we keep Melissa overnight?

By August, when my sister and her family arrived to
vacation with us for a week, Melissa's stays had
lengthened from overnight to two and three days. Even
with Gail, Hans, their six children and our four, it

seemed only natural that Melissa remain with us. We took her everywhere: picnicking, swimming, and sight-seeing. It was then I realized how much a part of my life she had become. Each time I returned her to the unit, I found it more difficult to leave. It was time to pray about bringing Melissa home to stay.

More than at any other time in my life, I felt the need to be certain of God's leading. Tony and I asked the Wednesday night prayer group at church to be praying with us, and we filled out the necessary papers at the Human Service Agency. Other preparations had to be made: shopping for baby clothes, diapers, bottles, and a crib. I took a new series of training classes on positioning and handling handicapped children, simple physical therapy routines, medications, and seizure training. At last everything was ready for Melissa's arrival. Or was it?

The phone rang early the morning of Melissa's homecoming. It was the nursing supervisor.

"Diane? This is Gary. I wonder if you would delay coming to the hospital until later this afternoon?"

"Of course. Anything wrong?" I asked uneasily.

"It's Katey. She died during the night. Things are pretty hectic around here right now."

It was several moments later, after hanging up the telephone, that I realized the impact of Gary's words.

Katey died!

In only a few hours I would be totally responsible for Melissa's care. What foolishness had made me think I could handle this kind of responsibility? I wasn't a doctor, not even a nurse. If Katey could die suddenly, so could Melissa. No amount of training would prepare me for the sudden death of a baby.

Certainly, as a nurse's aide in high school, I had witnessed death a few times. But that was different. The patients were elderly. Doctors, nurses, and equipment were only seconds away. What was I going to do alone with a fragile baby? Hadn't Melissa's sudden illness with pneumonia in July proven how frail she was?

Oh, Lord, please help me. I am so afraid! I know you brought Melissa into my life, but right now I am so frightened of her. What shall I do?

Trembling, I opened my Bible to the familiar words of Proverbs 3:5, 6: "Trust in the Lord with all your heart and do not rely on your own insight. In all your ways acknowledge him and he will make straight your paths."

As I read the words again and again, I began to understand that God was saying, "Trust me. Don't rely on your ability to understand. In all that you do, acknowledge me. I will be with you and I will show you the way."

If Melissa was frail and helpless, how much more so was I, without faith and trust. In a new way I realized that dependency on the Lord must be day by day.

Dr. Rice was completing Melissa's discharge examination when I arrived at the hospital. I was grateful for the opportunity to ask him the endless questions I now had since Katey's death.

"What tests have been done on Melissa and what do the results mean? . . . How long will she live? . . . What kinds of things is she likely to die from? . . . Is sudden infant death a possibility? . . . What would I do if she died at home? . . . Would you be willing to examine her every week?"

Dr. Rice patiently answered every question and assured me that he would see Melissa as often as I wished, until I felt more comfortable about caring for her. Although it was the first time we'd met, Dr. Rice's relaxed, unhurried manner gave me an immediate confidence in him. It seemed that this physician was a part of God's provision and I began to feel a bit more at peace.

Good-bye kisses were given to Melissa in rounds by the nursing staff and I was reminded of an upcoming appointment at the infant-stimulation program where I would be taking Melissa for weekly classes.

Once I was driving home, I turned to the baby lying on the seat beside me.

"Little one, our pastor says that children are a loan and a gift from God. Did you know that? *You* are a gift. For however long or short a time God has loaned you to us, Melissa, we're glad you're coming home."

6

Lessons with Nancy

Melissa slept soundly through her first night at home. When she finished her early morning bottle, I snuggled her against me and slipped back into bed. Cuddling her close, I thought how different she was from the boys when they were babies. Their round, ruddy cheeks had made them look like little pocket gophers. Melissa's features were milky white with just a hint of blush on her cheeks and lips. The boys had seemed to constantly wiggle and squirm, while Melissa was the quiet recipient of tender kisses as she lay in my arms.

I smoothed her lace-trimmed nightie and brushed her wispy strands of blond hair. With wonder, I considered the growing love in my heart. What mysterious process was it that bonded a woman to a child? Perhaps it was as unexplainable as my own mother, hundreds of miles away, knowing the precise moment to telephone.

"Hello, daughter," she greeted, delighted at my surprise.

MELISSA

"Mother! What in the world . . . do you realize you're phoning long distance in the morning?"

She giggled. "Oh, I just wanted to call and see if Lovey was in bed with you." (Some months earlier mother had sent me the book, *Lovey*, by Mary MacCracken, and through our conversations over the summer she had often referred to Melissa as Lovey.)

"How could you even ask such a question, mother, knowing I have a firm rule against taking babies into bed with me," I teased.

"Of course, dear. I realize that," she answered in mock seriousness. Following a brief silence we burst into simultaneous laughter.

"Oh, all right. I admit it. Melissa is right here, cuddled up in bed with me."

"Ah, ha!" Mom exclaimed gleefully. "I knew it!"

"Oh, mother," I said, glancing at the baby in my arms. "I wish you were here to see her. She truly is Lovey and Tony was right, she is beautiful."

"Put Melissa on the phone, honey," mom instructed. "Tell her that grandma wants to talk to her."

Placing the receiver next to Melissa's ear, I giggled at the scene; mother chatting long distance to this four-month-old baby.

"Melissa, grandma and grandpa can hardly wait to see you, sweetheart. We love you already. Did you know that? And when you come to visit, grandma is going to take you shopping. We're going to buy a balloon and a new dolly and . . ."

My eyes were brimming with tears by the time mother finished her conversation with Melissa.

"Mom," I said, swallowing hard. "Thanks for calling. You always know just the right thing to do. I love you."

"I love you, too, daughter. Kiss Melissa for me, will

you, dear?" Her voice quivered as she said good-bye.

The early autumn days passed quickly and with each weekly visit to Dr. Rice's office my concern about Melissa's health eased into confidence.

"You're doing a fine job, Diane. Melissa looks great. Keep up the good work," the doctor concluded following his examinations.

As reassuring as it was to know that Melissa was doing well medically, there was yet another area in which I had a great deal to learn; how to help her grow developmentally. It was time to begin the weekly classes at the Meyer Children's Rehabilitation Institute (MCRI).

Nancy, the infant-stimulation teacher sat cross-legged on the floor while Melissa reclined in an infant seat facing her. Unlike most classrooms for children, this starkly bare room had been divided into four simple cubicles. There were no colorful pictures on the walls, no shelves full of toys and books; nothing to distract the pupil from her teacher.

"The first thing we try to do when we see a child with severe multiple handicaps such as Melissa's," Nancy said, "is to try and determine just what abilities she *does* have; abilities she can use to interpret her environment and the things happening around her. We want to know how Melissa is able to control her environment, either by acting directly on it in the form of play or by communicating with us."

Nancy spread a soft blanket on the floor and asked me to take Melissa from the infant seat. As always, when being handled or moved, Melissa closed her eyes and wrinkled her face. Nancy's keen awareness caught the expression immediately.

"Diane, just a moment," she asked. "This is a good place to begin. Melissa is communicating with us by making a grim face. She's telling us that she isn't happy about being moved. Blind or visually impaired babies are sometimes defensive about being handled. Since they're unable to see what's about to happen, any movement may seem sudden and therefore unpleasant.

"To help Melissa anticipate," she continued, "I'd like you to cue her before picking her up. Would you put your hands under her, the way you ordinarily do when picking her up?"

As Nancy requested, I slid my right hand between Melissa's legs and under her bottom, placing my left hand behind her head to support its weight.

"OK. Now, before you lift, bounce her bottom a little. That's it. Explain what you're about to do; 'Pick up? Does Melissa want to be picked up?' Good. Do it once more. All right, lift her from the infant seat; slowly and smoothly."

With one fluid motion, Melissa was in my arms. "Look," I gasped in amazement. "She didn't close her eyes. She didn't even make a face."

"Great!" Nancy said, smiling. "Now, let's cue her for lay down by rocking her backwards. That's it, just a bit. Continue talking. Say, 'Lay down? Mommy is going to lay Melissa down.' Once more, and this time, all the way to the blanket. Perfect."

Again Melissa's eyes remained opened and she made no face. I was astonished at the difference the small cues had made, but also dismayed.

"Gosh, Nancy, when I think of how often I've just scooped her up into my arms without realizing what that must feel like . . ."

She patted my arm reassuringly. "Don't be too concerned. Even mommies with normal babies learn by trial and error what their babies' cries mean: 'I'm wet, I'm hungry, or I need to be burped.' The only real difference is that Melissa's signal is a wrinkled face instead of a loud cry.

"Does she vocalize for you, at home? Will she make sounds or coo?"

"No, she has begun to cry occasionally but it's still weak and faint, almost like a kitten."

"Mm hmm," Nancy murmured thoughtfully as she made notations on a yellow pad of paper. "And what about voluntary movement? Does Melissa ever kick her feet or move her arms?"

I shook my head. "She doesn't seem to move her legs at all. Sometimes she will open and close her hands a little but she's unable to hold or grasp."

I wondered momentarily about the notes Nancy was recording in response to my answers. If I expected she would be discouraged about Melissa's apparent weakness, I was wrong.

"Well," she said, sighing with determination. "That means we're going to give this little tyke some assistance."

She reached for a shocking-pink strip of yarn and a small, yellow rattle, gently tying the toy into Melissa's hand.

"Nonnutritive sucking is very important for babies. They seem to learn a great deal by putting things into their mouths. To help Melissa do that, we will lay her in a side position, with the dressed-up hand near her face. By touching the rattle to her lips a few times, perhaps we can encourage some independent mouthing."

Nancy placed the rattle against Melissa's mouth, moving it in a circular motion. Obligingly, Melissa parted her lips and moved her tongue against the toy, examining its smooth surface. I was beginning to feel like a first-time mother, fascinated with the intricate process of a baby's learning and exploring.

While Nancy played with Melissa on the floor, she continued talking:

"I'd like you to be thinking of a name sign to help Melissa identify you as mommy. It may be something similar to the sign language used by the deaf or simply a special way in which you touch her to let her know who you are. Have daddy and the rest of the family do the same."

"I think Tony has already begun to do that," I said, smiling. Every evening after work, he takes Melissa's hand, guides it across his moustache and says, 'Daddy's home, Melissa.' "

"Excellent! That's precisely what I mean. The sound of your voices, combined with a name sign and the particular way in which each of you handle her, will help Melissa to identify you.

"We also want to help Melissa identify the sounds she hears, so they will have meaning for her. For example, the sound of your footsteps coming into a room as meaning, 'Mommy is coming to pick me up.' In order to do that, you'll want to keep the background uncluttered with noise. Frequently, there is a temptation to play the radio or television in an effort to entertain a child who can do so little, but it's certainly the *wrong* thing to do for Melissa. Too much background will prevent her from sorting out a meaningful sound from the rest."

Nancy untied the rattle from Melissa's hand and once again positioned her in the infant seat. The large shoulder bag at her side reminded me of a Santa Claus backpack, overflowing with an odd collection of toys and objects. She rummaged through its contents, selecting a red and silver pinwheel.

"Vision seems to be an infant's most important tool for interpreting their little world. But because of problems within Melissa's eyes and damage to the central vision system in the brain, we know she will not see things as we do. Perhaps my pinwheel and other shiny objects will appear as light catchers. Sheets of colored tissue paper may be only blobs of color. Other things may be perceived as shadows or primitive shapes. By offering many kinds of shiny, colorful stimuli, we may be able to discover what Melissa likes, regardless of how it appears to her."

Blowing gently against the pinwheel, Nancy moved the spinning toy toward Melissa's face; back and forth, side to side. I leaned forward, eager for an indication that she was aware of the shiny object. When there was no response, Nancy paused and rested the pinwheel on her lap momentarily before repeating the procedure.

Melissa's eyes remained half closed. I was certain she had not seen the toy. Nancy's attempts with a chiming red ball were equally disappointing. Once again, the teacher made notations on the yellow pad of paper at her side. Turning back to Melissa, she jiggled the infant seat gently.

"Hey, Punkin', I have something pretty to show you. Look. Look what I have," she said, holding aloft a golden angel wind chime. Shining as they spun and danced, the angels produced a soft, tinkling melody.

Melissa stirred slightly. Slowly, her eyes began to open; wider and wider until she was fully alert. I held my breath. Was she merely waking from a nap? Or did she actually see the angels?

"Yes! *Good* baby," Nancy whispered. "Aren't they pretty?"

Melissa's eyes remained transfixed on the sparkling

figures even through the second and third trials. I applauded silently, afraid to break the magic of the moment. But inside, I cheered. *She did it! She did it!* Somehow, that small beginning seemed as significant as a baby's first step.

It was difficult to explain the intense excitement and fervent hope that that first infant-stimulation class sparked within me. Perhaps it was comparable to the experience of a nurse who, caring for a comatose patient, suddenly discovers that her patient is awakening from the coma. For it was one thing to love Melissa and to care for her physically, it was quite another to know she was aware of the events happening around her, and to believe that she *could* learn.

Somewhere, I had read:

The two greatest mistakes the parents of
a handicapped child can make are:
To believe that a miracle *will* happen . . . and,
To believe that a miracle *cannot* happen.

If Melissa would never walk or talk or even sit alone; if weeks and months passed before she reached the smallest goal, it mattered little. There was hope for a small, secret miracle tucked away in the pocket of my heart . . . that someday, Melissa would smile.

7

"Search Me, O God"

Nancy had referred Melissa's name to the MCRI screening clinic where a team of therapists would evaluate her needs and make corresponding recommendations. I was especially eager for the physical therapist's suggestions on ways to help Melissa grow in strength and the occupational therapist's ideas on improving feeding techniques.

The extra time I'd taken bathing and dressing Melissa was partly for the benefit of the Meyers' staff, but mostly because of a phone call I'd received the previous day.

"Diane? This is Sarah," she began hesitantly.

I had talked with Sarah only once, a few weeks earlier, when she and David had come to our home with an agency supervisor to sign the placement agreement. The three of us exchanged pleasantries, mutually unsure of the safety of closer topics. From the tone of Sarah's voice, I knew she was still uneasy.

"I, uh, received notice of Melissa's appointment and I . . . would you mind if I came along?"

"Mind? Of course not. I'd be happy to have you," I replied sincerely.

"You're certain I wouldn't be in the way or anything?"

"No, really. I'd be pleased if you'd join us," I assured her.

It was agreed we would meet at the institute at nine o'clock.

I thought again of our earlier meeting and the unsure, almost timid manner in which Sarah held the baby that morning; across her lap rather than cuddled close. I hoped the new pink dress and bonnet I'd chosen for Melissa to wear would help Sarah see her as I did—special and unique—but not so very different from other babies.

It was only during the drive to the institute that I began to have second thoughts. For the first time since Melissa had come to live with us, Sarah and I would be alone together. I knew it was bound to be an awkward situation. Doubts and questions played tag in my thoughts. I wondered who would carry Melissa—Sarah or me? I'd never faced a circumstance quite like this, but I already knew my answer to the question.

Of course *I* should carry Melissa. After all, I reasoned, I knew her better than anyone. Wouldn't she be more comfortable in my arms? I was the one who fed, bathed, and taught her. And it was I who spent long hours in doctor's offices, worried, and prayed for her. I loved Melissa. Didn't those facts in some way make *me* her mother?

Parking the car in front of the institute, I turned off the ignition key, sighed, and leaned back on the seat.

"Lord, just be with us this morning," I prayed.

The words had scarcely passed my lips when I felt an awesome awareness, the same sensation I'd often experi-

enced as a child, sensing my father's presence even before I'd turned to look behind me as he caught me in
some misdeed. God was *indeed* with me, as I'd asked, but
more than that, he'd heard every unspoken thought.

As clearly as if he'd taken his finger and written in the
dust on the windshield of the car, I saw the contents of my
heart: selfishness, possessiveness, fear.

"Yes, I am afraid, Father; afraid that if Sarah holds and
carries Melissa, she will love her and want to take her
home. But, I love Melissa, too! And Sarah's presence at
the evaluation will be an all too real reminder that Melissa
is not *my* baby.

In the silence, I heard his reminder:

Love endures long and is patient and kind.
Love is never envious and does not boil over with
jealousy.
It is not boastful or vainglorious and does not display
itself haughtily.
It is not conceited, arrogant, or inflated with pride.
It is not rude and does not act unbecomingly.
Love—God's love in you—does not insist on its own
rights or its own way, for it is not self-seeking.
Love bears up under anything; it is ever ready to be-
lieve the best of every person.
Its hopes do not fade under any circumstances.
It endures everything without weakening.
Love never fails.

(Adapted from the *Amplified* Version.)

But, God! I wanted to cry out. You don't understand. I
do want to love Sarah, I just can't! What if . . . The
sentence went unfinished. At once, I remembered an
Old Testament story in which two women brought a baby
to wise King Solomon, each claiming to be the child's

mother. One of the women would have kept the baby at all cost. But the other woman, the child's real mother, offered to give up the baby she loved rather than see it harmed.

There was little doubt which type of mother I was. Once again, I prayed, but this time it was a prayer of surrender to God's will and of asking his forgiveness.

Taking Melissa from the car seat beside me, I entered the building where Sarah was already waiting. I took a deep breath and smiled as she rose from her chair. I hadn't noticed before how much she and Melissa looked alike. They shared the same fresh complexion, deep blue eyes, and strawberry-blond hair.

Sarah greeted us nervously. I resisted a sudden impulse to hug her and assure her that, somehow, everything would be all right. Instead, I placed Melissa in her arms, purposely making an excuse to leave the two of them alone.

Standing at the receptionist's desk, I couldn't resist watching their reflection in the window. I observed while Sarah carefully unwrapped Melissa's blanket and untied her bonnet. Slowly, the corners of her mouth turned upward into a smile when she saw the new pink dress and shiny size-0 shoes.

What words was she speaking softly to the baby we shared, I wondered. She stroked Melissa's cheek and brushed her hair until it lay smoothly in place. I turned from the window and glanced at the clock.

"It's time to go, Sarah," I said, reaching for her coat and draping it over my arm as we started down the hall.

"Do you think Melissa has grown any?" I asked.

She lowered her eyes and looked at the baby in her arms. "Oh, yes! Her face is beginning to fill out and she's finally getting hair."

I nodded. "She certainly knows what she likes to eat. Carrots and peaches are her favorites. When they're on the menu she smacks loudly and hardly misses a bite. Each spoonful of anything else has to be put back into her mouth two or three times."

"Really? She knows what she likes to eat?"

"Absolutely," I replied.

Sarah was noticeably silent for a time and I wondered if I'd said something wrong. It was then I realized Sarah must have had as many doubts and inner conflicts about our being together as I had had, perhaps even more.

As we approached the spacious room filled with parallel bars and adaptive equipment of all types, I was pleased to see that Duane, an old friend, was assigned to evaluate Melissa. He'd also been Lori's physical therapist. We renewed our acquaintance and I introduced him to Sarah.

"And this little gal must be Melissa," he said. "All right, young lady, let's have a look at you and see what we can do to help you."

With the confidence that came from years of handling handicapped children, Duane carried Melissa to a large, green tumbling mat and seated himself on the floor next to her. Sarah and I drew folding chairs to one side.

With expertise, the therapist moved Melissa's limbs through the range of motion, testing the flexibility of each joint. His raised eyebrows indicated he was puzzled by her limpness.

"Has she always been this flaccid?" he asked, glancing first at Sarah, then at me. We both nodded.

"Well, there's certainly no concerns about tightness in the joints or heel cords at this time."

Duane continued by tapping his fingers on Melissa's limbs, looking for involuntary reflexes. There were

65

none. For a time, Sarah and I quietly observed his various attempts to stimulate Melissa's arms and legs into movement.

Every nerve and muscle in my own body tensed as if somehow, the ability to move could be transmitted to the small baby on the mat. Again and again, inwardly, I urged. *Come on, Melissa. You can do it. Please give us some indication the message is getting through and show us your body can respond.* It was an extravagant wish, wanting to see Melissa move her arms and legs as other babies did. But she remained motionless. Her only response to the therapist's tactics was a faint, weak cry of protest. Two tiny tears rolled down her cheeks.

I glanced at Sarah. Her lips were trembling. She was struggling, trying not to cry. There was a thin, white line where her teeth had bitten hard into her bottom lip. She swallowed several times.

"I . . . didn't think she could even cry. I've never *seen* her cry." Sobbing, she fumbled in her purse, searching for a tissue.

"I'm sorry . . . it's . . . sometimes . . . it's still very hard."

"I understand," I said, reaching for her hand, giving it a firm, brief squeeze. "Sometimes when Melissa cries, I cry, too."

A secretary interrupted with a note asking me to meet with the social worker in her office. Reluctantly, I left Sarah with Duane and Melissa to finish that portion of the evaluation.

For thirty minutes I restlessly answered questions in the social worker's cramped office. "How many in your family? How long has Melissa been with you? What do you understand about the reasons for her being placed in foster care? How long do you expect she will remain with your family? . . ."

The questions seemed to drag on and on. I tried telling myself the social worker was a very nice lady who was only doing her job, but I was relieved when the interview ended and I was directed to Dr. Trembath's office where Sarah and Melissa were waiting.

"Well, Mrs. B., how are you?" Dr. Trembath asked, offering me a chair. "It's been four or five years, hasn't it, since you were here with Lori? It's good to see you again."

"Thank you. I see you've already met Melissa and Sarah."

"Yes, I was about to ask mom if she'd undress the little one so I can examine her," he said, turning to Sarah. She hesitated before answering, "No, I . . . I'd rather not. Diane had better undress her. I don't . . ." her voice drifted off.

"Tell you what, mom," Dr. Trembath offered kindly. "Since the social worker is waiting for an opportunity to talk with you, why don't you see her while I have a look at Melissa?"

Sarah seemed to welcome the suggestion. After handing Melissa to me, she closed the door quietly behind her.

Dr. Trembath turned back to the papers on his desk. "Let's see, Melissa is nearly six months old. What kind of things is she doing now, Diane?"

"She seems to be increasing in alertness," I answered. "And generally is awake for longer periods of time. She's begun to cry a bit when she's hungry or wants to be repositioned."

"OK, Anything else?"

I thought for a moment, then noticed the position of Melissa's thumb, tucked between the first two fingers of her hand. Sign language was often used with our retarded foster children. Melissa's hand was formed in the deaf sign T, often used for toilet training. I had a mischievous idea.

"Yes, there is one other thing. Melissa signs for 'potty.' "

Dr. Trembath cautiously turned his head and stared at me.

"She signs for potty?" he asked, incredulous. I was delighted I'd taken him in.

"Mm hmm," I answered soberly. "I'd like you to write that down in her chart."

He stared at me, unable to believe I was really serious. Slowly, I lifted Melissa's hand, showing him the position of her fingers.

"See, it's true. I can't help it if she's only six months old, she *does* sign for potty."

Dr. Trembath rolled his eyes and roared with laughter. "Diane, if I put that in her chart, they would revoke my license to practice medicine! Signs for potty, huh?" he said, still shaking his head at the very idea.

I removed Melissa's clothes for the examination.

"Any problems, Diane?" the doctor asked. "Any concerns?"

"Only one. Lately I've wondered if Melissa was beginning to have some seizure activity." Almost on cue, Melissa tilted her head back slightly and opened her eyes wide.

Dr. Trembath confirmed my suspicion; she *was* having a seizure. As yet, it was mild. My heart sank just a little. I'd cared for children who'd had as many as a hundred seizures a day and others who were so heavily medicated they were lethargic and unresponsive. No one could promise Melissa's seizures would remain mild and infrequent.

"I'll phone Dr. Rice and confer with him. I'm sure he'll want to prescribe some medication, but there's little else we doctors can do."

"I'm grateful for your help, Dr. Trembath, but I also believe in prayer. What doctors can't do, God *can.*"

"Mrs. B.," he said, looking earnestly into my eyes, "of all the things you have going for you, hang on to that one!"

I didn't see Sarah again before leaving the institute but I couldn't get her out of my thoughts. That evening after supper I shared the day's events with Tony.

"I know I can't begin to understand what Sarah's been through but I wish I could help her, encourage her in some way. I've been thinking of asking her to go out for breakfast some morning."

Tony agreed with the idea and suggested, "Let's pray for her and David right now."

As we'd done with many of our foster children in the past, we held Melissa in our arms and prayed for her parents.

"God, where would *we* be if someone hadn't cared enough to pray for us in times of need. We think of Melissa's parents right now, Lord, and their suffering. Because you have always been a Father, you understand a parent's heart, and hurt. We're grateful we have a God who cares about our pain. We ask you to help Melissa's parents at this time. Be with them according to their need."

The Baumgartners
with Doug (far left)
and Lori—fall, 1974

Lori, Diane, and Doug—fall, 1974

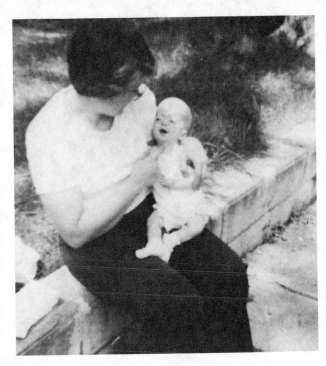

Diane and Melissa—
a very special baby

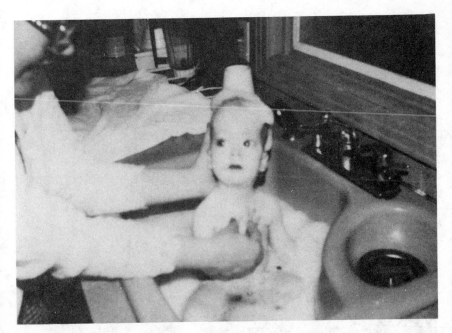

Sign for bath

Melissa at seven months

Grandma and
Grandpa
Braunstein
with 'Liss

Tony, Melissa,
and Diane

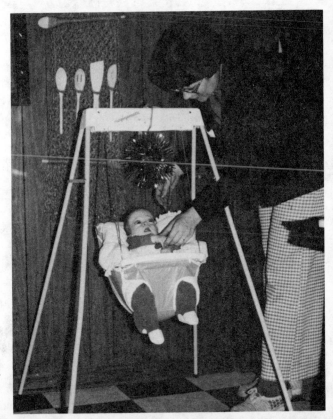

A new hand
in ours

Melissa playing the role of baby Jesus in Cameron's school play

Making daddy
thumbprint
cookies
in Rob's
chef's hat

Melissa turns one

Vacationing
in the
Black Hills

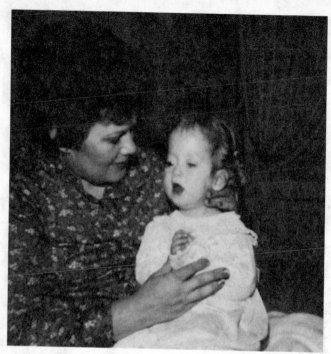

"Now I lay me
down to sleep . . ."

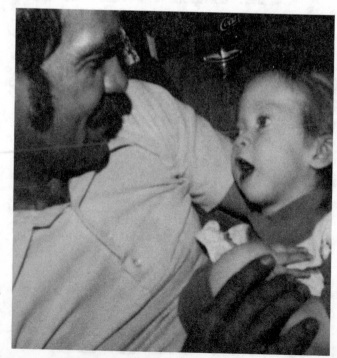

A daughter puts
a song in
your heart

Our bathing
beauty

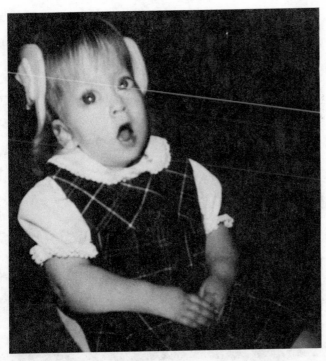

Melissa in her
new spinal
support chair

Listening to Christmas music through headphones

Relaxing on
our sun deck

Nap time

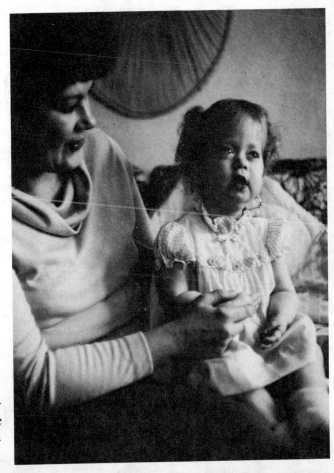

Waiting for daddy
to come home
from work

8

Reaching Out

With the chilly dampness of late October, Melissa grew increasingly congested. Even a minor cold was cause for serious concern, and I knew pneumonia could be fatal. Recent clinic visits with the battery of specialists involved in Melissa's care did little to relieve my anxiety.

The neurologist, urologist, orthopedist, and neurosurgeon made hurried impersonal examinations and left me with little doubt they saw no value in providing treatment other than simple maintenance care. Their expectation that Melissa would live only a few months, perhaps less, was apparent. Hopelessness permeated those clinic visits.

It was the weekly office visits with Dr. Rice that always seemed to put things into proper perspective.

"Melissa's lungs sound much better today, Diane," he said, following a week of upper-respiratory problems. "What have you been doing, praying for her?"

I answered affirmatively. He smiled with a twinkle in his eye.

"Good medical intervention! Keep that up Diane," he encouraged.

I had suspected when Dr. Rice held Melissa's hand in his and seemed to be pondering a decision about her care that he was also praying for her.

At Dr. Rice's suggestion, I made an appointment with an opthalmologist to determine the cause of Melissa's eyes being enlarged. Dr. Bush swiftly reached his diagnosis.

"Melissa has glaucoma," he advised.

"Glaucoma?" I questioned. "Pressure in the eyes? But isn't that a problem with elderly people?"

"There is more than one kind of glaucoma; Melissa has a congenital form. The cause and treatment are quite different from the condition in aged folks. Surgery is necessary in this case to relieve the pressure in the eye, but I must inform you the procedures are still somewhat experimental since we see only one or two cases like this each year. And I can't assure you that our efforts will be successful."

"And if the problem isn't corrected?" I asked cautiously.

The pressure in the eye would result in continued damage to the optic nerve. There is a possibility, though remote, that the eyes would ulcerate, necessitating removal."

I felt sickened at the thought. Dr. Bush scheduled Melissa's surgery for November 1, ten days away. Since Sarah and I were planning to meet for breakfast the following morning, I tucked the surgical permission form requiring her signature into my purse.

She waved from a distant booth as I entered the restaurant with Melissa. I noted gratefully that she had selected a secluded corner where we would be able to talk without interruption.

"Good morning," I offered. "Sorry I'm late. I'm beginning to feel as if my entire life is fifteen minutes behind schedule."

She chuckled. "It's all right. I haven't been waiting long."

Melissa was sleeping soundly when I placed her in the booth beside Sarah.

"Gosh, she looks so pretty," Sarah said wistfully. "It's easy to see you take good care of her."

"I told her we were going to visit mommy today and gave her firm instructions to be wide awake, but as you can see she didn't pay a bit of attention," I said.

A perky, petite waitress brought a steaming pot of coffee and took our orders.

Wondering where to begin, I chose the infant-stimulation classes Melissa had been attending as a likely place to start the conversation. I was certain Sarah would share my enthusiasm over Melissa's progress. Instead she looked bewildered.

"You mean, you actually think she's *changing?*" she asked.

I was taken aback by the question. "Yes. I do. The progress is small, but real!"

Sarah glanced at Melissa, sleeping beside her, then back at me but made no comment. For a moment I felt as if she was actually feeling sorry for *me*. I decided not to mention the subject any further.

The waitress returned with our orders and refilled the coffee cups.

"Would you like to pray before we eat, Sarah?" I asked. She nodded. As we bowed our heads, I reached for her hand, and held it as we prayed.

"Thank you for this food we are about to eat, Lord. And for the opportunity to be with Sarah this morning. Father, you know all the circumstances that have brought our lives together. More than anyone, you understand Sarah's hurt and grief. I pray especially for her now, that she might come to know how much you love her. Bless Melissa and use her life for good, for we ask all these things in the name of Jesus. Amen."

Simultaneously reaching for a Kleenex, Sarah and I burst into laughter. "We must be a sight," she said. "The two of us bawling and blowing our noses."

I had to agree.

"I feel so silly," Sarah sighed. "I thought I was over this crying weeks ago. But ever since the evaluation last week, I can't seem to stop crying."

"It must have been a hard day for you."

"I guess I wasn't prepared to . . . see you as Melissa's mother. David and I had agreed that a foster home would be better for her than a hospital, realizing no matter how good the care is, every baby needs a family. But I guess when it came right down to it, I suppose I didn't really believe anyone would even *want* to take her."

She swished the orange juice in the bottom of her glass. I waited for her to continue. "At first, I felt so fortunate to have Melissa with someone like you. I still do. It's just that in the hospital it was the *nurses* who took care of her. It was a pretty nonthreatening situation.

"But last week, when I saw you and Melissa together it was obvious *you* were her mother. You . . . you're so comfortable with her. You laugh and joke about her and treat her just as if she were normal. I can't do that. All I feel is hopelessness and pity."

"You mustn't compare yourself to me. It isn't fair.

Tony and I have foster parented many handicapped children. It isn't so new or overwhelming for us, as it must be for you. Besides, I'm not grieving and hurting as you are. Five years ago, if I had given birth to a child like Melissa, I may have felt no differently than you do."

"But I'm just plain frightened of her," Sarah protested.

"Of course you are. I was, too, at first. In fact, the first few nights after bringing her home, I hardly slept. I was worried that she would smother, choke, or any number of other possibilities."

"Really? You felt that way? But how did you overcome it?"

"Some of the fear and uncertainty simply disappeared in time as I grew to know Melissa better and recognized that what was normal for other babies may not be the norm for her. But mostly, the peace and confidence I needed came from knowing that God holds Melissa's life in his hands. He loves and cares about her even more than we do."

Sarah turned and looked pensively out the restaurant window. "I wish I could have faith. I do want to believe, but it's so hard. I remember soon after Melissa was born, someone said to me, 'How could there be a loving God when things like this happen to innocent babies?' Why *did* it happen? I had good prenatal care. I didn't take drugs or drink or do any of the things they say cause birth defects."

"In a sense, I guess you could say it began with Adam and Eve. Until they disobeyed God, there was no sickness or disease. But when sin entered this world, so did suffering and death."

Sarah lowered her eyes and stirred her coffee. "I keep asking myself if God is punishing me for something."

"Sarah, I can assure you God did not cause this to

happen. He's not the author of sickness and disease and he doesn't hurt babies to punish you or anyone else. I don't know the answer as to why he allows certain things to happen, but I do know he loves you."

"But what if I am doing the wrong thing by not bringing Melissa home? Am I just dumping my problem onto someone else? Will this keep happening to me?"

"What would you *like* to do? Have you considered bringing Melissa home for visits?"

She hesitated a long while before answering. "Yes, I have thought about it but, I don't know. Do you think I could handle it?"

"Of course you can do it. I could help you with the things I've learned. I'm sure you would do just fine."

She looked at Melissa and was silent for a long while. "You know, I've never even been alone with her."

It was almost time to leave when I remembered the surgical permission form in my purse. I told Sarah of the visit with the ophthalmologist and the need for surgery. We agreed Melissa's first visit would take place as soon as she had recovered from the operation.

As we said good-bye, Sarah told me it was the first time she'd been able to open up and talk with anyone since Melissa's birth, and she was feeling much better.

Our visit also left me with a warm feeling. It was only after the boys and Melissa were bedded down for the night that the second thoughts returned.

"How did it go today, with Sarah?" Tony asked.

"To use an old cliche," I answered, flopping across the bed, "I think I'm about to discover what it feels like to be hung with my own rope!"

Tony looked puzzled and waited for me to explain. "I like Sarah very much. She was remarkably open and honest, especially considering the circumstances. I'd like to be her friend and help her. It surprises me how badly I care that Sarah likes Melissa—knowing that if she *does* love her, we might lose her. I feel like I'm being put through a paper shredder! I'm excited about the possibility of Sarah's taking Melissa home and yet it's the thing I dread happening most. It would be like losing our own child."

"Honey," Tony began, "perhaps those emotions are the very ones that will enable you and Sarah to be friends and understand one another. In a way, you are facing similar struggles. She is grateful that you love Melissa like a mother, and yet that very fact causes her pain."

Tony turned out the lights and crawled under the covers. In the darkness, I asked the question I'd been afraid to voice.

God, is this the purpose for which Melissa was brought into my life—that I might help Sarah to take her home? Lord, if it is your will, please help me to accept it.

9

Home Visit

For the third time in less than an hour, I sat up in bed and looked at the clock. It was 4:30 A.M. Melissa would be in the operating room in four more hours. Relenting to the swarm of thoughts that persisted in keeping me awake, I tossed back the covers.

Why hadn't I remembered to tell the anesthetist last night to be certain Melissa was lying on her side in the recovery room to allow secretions to drain from her mouth? How could I have forgotten to tell him she was hypothermic and would need to be wrapped warmly in a blanket? How many other things had I overlooked?

As I showered and dressed, I made a mental list of information regarding Melissa's care. It was 5:10 when I roused Tony and told him I was leaving for the hospital.

"Give 'Liss a big kiss for daddy," he said. "I'll join you as soon as the boys leave for school."

Even in the semidarkness of the hospital, I could see Melissa's enormous blue eyes as I tiptoed into her room.

MELISSA

She looked to and fro as if awaiting my arrival. Silently, I lowered the crib rail, gave the sign for *mommy* and slipped her into my arms.

"Good morning, most beautiful girl in the whole wide world! Were you waiting for mommy?" I asked. Melissa responded with a humming sound I knew must have meant yes.

Not wanting to wake three-month-old Justin who shared Melissa's room, I tucked a soft afghan around her and strolled toward the nurses' station.

"Melissa and I will be in the parents' lounge," I told a plump night nurse.

Turning down the darkened corridor, I pushed through the heavy swinging doors. The waiting room was empty. After drawing the thick drapes, I snuggled Melissa close and curled up in the window seat. Light was just beginning to dawn on the horizon.

In hushed tones, I talked with Melissa about the operation and reminded her of the friends who were praying. I assured her that daddy and I would be nearby, but most important of all, Jesus would be at her side every moment. From my pocket, I withdrew a miniature book, *Meditations for Mothers,* and read the selected portions of Scripture.

Melissa searched my face as I read. Occasionally, she closed her eyes and breathed a deep sigh. I knew, even though she could not understand the verses, her spirit was receiving God's Word.

As morning broke, activity in the hospital increased. In the distance, hungry babies cried for bottles, toddlers called for their mothers, and breakfast carts clanged in the hallways. Nurses and interns scurried through the change of shift.

Even before the nurse told me, I knew it was time.

Once more, I pressed my cheek against Melissa's and drank in the faint fragrance of baby lotion. In rhythm with the approaching surgical cart, I kissed her again and again.

A green-gowned figure appeared in the doorway.

"Ready, Melissa?" he asked.

Reluctantly, I relinquished her to the cart. She seemed dwarfed by its size. Courage seeped from me as if through some freshly opened wound.

The surgical nurse removed Melissa's frilly nightie and tied on a stiff, open-backed hospital gown. A lump sought its way to my throat. I swallowed hard, trying not to cry.

"If you like, you may ride with us in the elevator," the nurse offered. I accepted gratefully.

Through the bars on the side of the cart, I held Melissa's hand as the elevator descended. Fifth floor, fourth, third, second. Time for one last kiss on the tiny hand that encircled my finger. The elevator opened and the cart was whisked away.

In a moment, the door closed and I stood alone. Only a small pink nightie remained in my hand. The waiting began.

At 8:30 I signed the register in the surgical waiting room and poured a cup of coffee. In a quiet corner of the room, an elderly man fingered a rosary. A young couple played a game of cards at the round table. Two women, dressed in hospital auxiliary smocks, hung macrame planters in the windows. I fingered through a stack of magazines, but found nothing to distract my thoughts.

Shortly after nine, Tony arrived. Love welled up in me at the sight of him. He kissed me lightly on the forehead.

"How's our girl?" he asked.

"She was wide awake when I arrived and seemed to be

waiting for me. I asked them not to give a preop anesthetic since she wouldn't cry or be frightened when she left me."

"Maybe they should have a preop anesthetic for mothers who cry and are frightened when the baby leaves," Tony said, squeezing my shoulder.

As time went by, one by one the others in the room were called to the receptionist's desk and told their loved one was out of surgery. Still we waited. At eleven, my patience was exhausted. I insisted the receptionist phone the surgery floor and inquire about Melissa. The only information given was that Melissa was still in surgery.

Dr. Bush had said the operation would take about an hour. Allowing for thirty minutes in the preop room, she should have been finished long ago. Another thirty minutes passed before Dr. Bush, still dressed in his surgical greens, breezed into the waiting room.

"Melissa is in recovery. We had some delay getting started. Turnover time for the operating room was slower than anticipated and we had difficulty getting an IV started, but the surgery went well."

I sighed with relief.

"Her heart rate and blood pressure remained stable. Now we'll just have to wait and see if we've corrected the problem. Any questions?"

"Just one," Tony said. "When can we see her?"

Dr. Bush glanced at his watch. "Shouldn't be more than another half hour in recovery. Then she'll be taken back to her room."

I telephoned Sarah; then Tony and I ate a hurried breakfast and returned to Melissa's room. An hour passed. Periodically, a nurse stuck her head in the doorway to smile and say, "It shouldn't be much longer." I paced the floor, thinking of all that could have gone wrong. When another thirty minutes went by and there was still no sign of Melissa, I pleaded:

"Please, won't you phone and make certain everything is all right?"

The report came back, "Melissa is fine. They just want to be sure she is fully awake."

Then it occurred to me. Of course! Why hadn't I thought of it before? They were waiting for Melissa to cry and kick as other babies did. And when she lay very quiet and still, they must have assumed she was still anesthetized. I shared my realization with Tony and we laughed with relief. Everything was going to be all right.

We waited near the elevator and escorted the cart carrying Melissa back to her room. My heart nearly broke at the sight of her. Metal shields had been taped across her eyes. Intravenous tubing protruded from a small vein in her neck. She looked even tinier and more helpless.

After tucking her into bed, the floor nurse took her vital signs and temperature. "Ninety-six!" She gasped, and rushed down the hall for an armful of warm blankets. Gradually, Melissa's icy cold body warmed to an adequate ninety-eight degrees.

For the three days she remained in the hospital, I found it necessary to feed her drop by drop through an oral syringe. She was badly congested and simply too weak to suck.

At home, her temperature fluctuated between ninety-seven and one-hundred-three degrees. Total daily intake remained at eight ounces. Dr. Rice's examination two days later confirmed my fear. Melissa had pneumonia. After some discussion, we agreed that as long as possible I would care for her at home. Unless oxygen was necessary I could provide all that a hospital would.

MELISSA

What I had nearly run from months earlier (responsibility for Melissa's well-being), I could now relinquish to no one. Faith had been granted at the precise moment I needed it.

Hour after hour, as I fed Melissa each small drop, I waited for the combination of prayer, medicine, and nourishment to give evidence that healing had begun. At times during those hours I sensed a tangible awareness of God's presence.

One day stretched into another as I recorded her progress:

Monday. Daily intake is twelve and one-half ounces.
Tuesday. Melissa sleeping continuously; fourteen ounces.
Wednesday. Congestion beginning to loosen; thirteen ounces.
Thursday. Awake one hour this evening; fourteen ounces.
Friday. Sounds much better today; seventeen ounces.
Saturday. Sucking one ounce from bottle before tiring; twenty ounces. Awake three hours today.
Sunday. Chest sounds clear. Alert and awake all afternoon. Sucking continues to improve; twenty-four ounces.

It was two weeks after surgery when I telephoned Sarah to say Melissa was feeling well again and was ready for a home visit. We talked at length about her care and covered any problems that might arise. Wanting things to go smoothly, I made a schedule for Melissa's daily routine and drew each dose of medication into small oral syringes. Carefully, I folded several tiny undershirts, nighties, and dresses and placed them in an overnight case.

Moments before Sarah arrived, I decided to add extra diapers and formula. A winter storm was approaching. Only a year earlier, a blizzard closed all city streets, making travel impossible for three days. Snowflakes had already begun to fall when the doorbell rang.

Sarah appeared relaxed and chatted almost casually as we went over Melissa's schedule and I gave last-minute instructions about the medications.

While I zipped Melissa into her pink snowsuit, the boys carried the diaper bag and overnight case to the car.

"Don't be upset. There's no need to worry. She'll be fine," I told myself, watching from the window as the car rounded the corner and turned out of sight.

The weather worsened during the night. I watched its activity anxiously the next day while drifting from one meaningless task to another. The house seemed so empty. I wondered how the absence of one small baby could make such a difference. Could I adjust once again to being without her? What had my life been like before Melissa? I couldn't remember.

It was late afternoon when Sarah returned. The snow was blowing fiercely now, making the streets hazardous. With Melissa returned safely to my arms, Sarah scurried off, wanting to reach home before dark.

Although she gave no indication of how the visit had gone, I felt unexplainably certain that Melissa would be going home to stay.

10

A Song in My Heart

The boys laughed excitedly as they carried Christmas boxes up the basement steps. We had never put the tree up this early before. It was only the Saturday following Thanksgiving. But there seemed to be such a holiday spirit in the air we could wait no longer.

When the last bulb had been hung and the final strands of tinsel draped over the branches, Tony moved Melissa's chair closer. Everyone was in their place for the first lighting of the tree. The boys, especially, were delighted by Melissa's wide-eyed response to the twinkling spectacle.

In addition to the tree-trimming party, the boys insisted Melissa be included in all family activities: Shannon's ROTC inspection at the junior high, Rob's football games, Chuck's piano recital at school, and Cameron's YMCA basketball games. With great pride they showed her off to friends and bragged about her to anyone who expressed even a mild interest.

MELISSA

When Tony and the boys surprised me with a bouquet of flowers one Saturday afternoon in mid-December, it was Melissa they chose to make the presentation. While I worked in the kitchen I heard their suppressed giggles. Frequently, they called, "Mom, don't come in here." Finally I was beckoned to the living room.

In the center of the room Melissa had been positioned in her car seat holding a single blue carnation. From the expression on her face, she seemed to know she was in on the secret.

"Look, mom. I have a surprise for you," someone hidden out of sight spoke the words for her.

Tears filled my eyes, as I went to Melissa and kissed her.

"Did you pick this for mommy? Oh, thank you, sweetheart!"

Together we sniffed the fragrant flower she held. It was only then that Tony and the boys appeared with the remainder of the colorful bouquet. No-occasion flowers always seem to be the best kind.

By the time the last batch of Christmas goodies was baked a few days later, a new tradition was born; thumbprint cookies. In addition to stars, bells, and snowflakes, the boys helped Melissa make a surprise for daddy. Before each pan of sugar cookies was popped into the oven, they made certain at least one of them contained a tiny thumbprint.

Although every other cookie was eventually covered with thick red or green frosting, one corner of the thumbprint cookies remained untouched. Daddy had no difficulty discovering which ones were made by Melissa especially for him.

For days I had put Melissa's last eye appointment out of my thoughts. Dr. Bush had found the pressure elevated, indicating the need for further surgery. Since there was no immediate opening in the operating schedule we postponed the hospitalization until after the holidays. But a phone call from Dr. Bush's nurse required a hasty change of plans.

"There's been a cancellation on the twentieth. Doctor would like to admit Melissa tomorrow afternoon. Surgery will be at 9:00 the following morning. If all goes well, she'll be home in time for Christmas."

I was especially thankful now that Christmas preparations were finished earlier than usual. It seemed as if God had taken care of even the smallest detail.

The wind howled and faint swirls of snow encircled my feet as I hurried from the parking lot to the hospital across the street. I glanced at my watch under the street lamp. Ten till seven. My progress had been slowed by the snowdrifted streets, but there was still plenty of time before Melissa would be taken to surgery.

I shook the melting snow from my coat, opened the door silently and entered her room. The crib was empty! How could it be empty? I stared at it in disbelief. She couldn't be gone. It was too early. Frantically I ran to the nurses' station. *Please, don't let her be gone before I've seen her this morning.* My heart sank when the nurse verified my fear!

"She left only moments ago. There was a change of plans and at the last minute they moved her up on the operating schedule."

I said nothing, resisting the temptation to snap angrily back. Why couldn't hospitals get organized enough to do things on schedule? What gave them the right to take her early, anyway?

MELISSA

Agitated, I walked the floor in the surgical waiting room. It was less than an hour when I was motioned to the receptionist's desk.

"The surgical intern would like to talk with you in Dr. Bush's clinic upstairs," she said calmly.

My heart pounded furiously as I raced to his office. Why hadn't Dr. Bush simply phoned to say Melissa was in recovery? Or why didn't he come to the waiting room, as he had done last time? Something had gone wrong!

The intern rose from his desk as I stormed into the office. It seemed an eternity before he spoke. When he did, I could scarcely hear his words for the hammering in my ears.

"Mrs. Baumgartner, I'm sorry. I've made a serious mistake. I put the wrong drops into Melissa's eyes. One type of drop is used to dilate the pupil, another to contract it. Because of my error, it will be necessary to wait until tomorrow to do the surgery."

I almost fainted with relief. Melissa was all right. I was so grateful I couldn't even be angry with the dismayed young intern. I almost felt sorry for him. He walked with me back to Melissa's room, apologizing every step of the way.

Everything went smoothly the following morning. Melissa even seemed to be awake when they returned her from the recovery room. Contentedly, she sucked on her pacifier while I decorated her crib with shiny foil Christmas ornaments. I had to admit the final result was a bit gaudy, but it did erase the cold, sterile feeling of the hospital.

Sarah and Grandma Jean suggested exchanging Melissa's Christmas gifts at the hospital. The decorated crib and small gold tree I'd placed on the nightstand gave the room a party air.

Grandma had selected a colorful mobile that played Brahm's "Lullaby." Sarah's present was a curly gray poodle with a red bow around its neck.

When wound, it turned its head to the tune of, "How Much Is That Doggie in the Window?" I waited till last to present Melissa's gift to them; a recent photograph. There were hugs and thanks all 'round before we said good night. Sarah wished Melissa a Merry Christmas and said she'd call soon.

As promised, Melissa was home for her first Christmas. With the holidays over and the surgery behind us, our normal routine resumed. The boys returned to school and Melissa once again attended the infant-stimulation classes.

"My *goodness,* this child has grown," Nancy exclaimed, "How much does she weigh now?"

"A whopping twelve pounds," I answered proudly. "She gained four ounces this month."

"Not bad for eight months old, I'd say," Nancy smiled.

"Diane, let's begin today by having you lay Melissa on the blanket and playing some games with her. Show me what you're doing at home."

Nancy observed while I played patty-cake with Melissa. When I paused between games, Melissa tossed her head slightly from side to side, vocalizing several sounds.

"Excellent!" Nancy commented. "Melissa not only responds when you talk to her, she's trying to elicit conversation when you're silent."

Once again, I took Melissa's hand in mine. Giving the sign for the high-low stretching game we played, I rubbed her hands across her tummy. Immediately, her mouth opened wide in recognition of what was to come.

"She almost looks as if she's smiling, doesn't she?" I

asked, directing Nancy's attention to Melissa's expression.

"She *is* smiling," Nancy said firmly. "Often blind babies' first smiles are openmouthed, because they are unable to see turned-up lips."

"You mean it's not my imagination?" I had to be certain.

"Positively. She is smiling," Nancy confirmed. "It appears to me you two have something special going on."

I could scarcely contain my joy the remainder of class. The secret petition of my heart had been answered; Melissa had learned to smile.

The office visit with Dr. Rice that afternoon put the crowning touch on the day. Following his examination, he tucked the stethoscope back into his pocket and said: "Everything looks great. I'll see you two in a month."

"A month!" I repeated. "Don't you mean next week?"

He shook his head. "Melissa is progressing so well, I think it's time we discontinued the weekly checkups."

I was pleased with Dr. Rice's decision. But driving home, I wondered about the significance of the way things now seemed to be coming together, as if tied into a neat little package. Perhaps too neat.

It was late January when Sarah telephoned. Immediately, I noted a serious tone in her voice.

"Diane, is this a good time to talk?" she asked. I could tell she wasn't calling just to chat.

"David and I have been talking. We don't know how you and Tony would feel about this but . . ."

My thoughts raced ahead of her words. They'd reached a decision. I could sense it. Melissa would be going home. I was amazed at the calmness I felt inside. I wasn't going to panic after all. "Thank you, Lord," I breathed, "for having helped me to accept this."

Sarah's words caught my attention once again.

". . . and we know that you and Tony love her in a way we've been unable to. If you would like to adopt Melissa, we will relinquish custody."

I was stunned. They weren't going to take Melissa home. We could adopt her. It was the last thing I had expected to hear; and the best.

Minutes later, I was dancing around the room with Melissa in my arms, laughing, crying, and thanking God, all at the same time. I was almost bursting to share the news with someone—everyone! It was all I could do to restrain myself until Tony arrived home.

I glanced at the clock every few minutes. Finally, the car pulled into the drive. He called, "Hello," then as always went directly to Melissa. Taking her hand in his, he guided it across the moustache, giving the sign for daddy.

"How's daddy's girl today? Did you miss dad?"

Melissa sighed.

"You did? How about a big kiss for daddy?"

Her mouth and tongue moved in anticipation.

"Oh, such good kisses. Dad loves Melissa's kisses."

Standing erect, Tony turned to me. "Hi, honey," he said, planting a light kiss on my cheek.

"It's about time," I teased. "Seems that I've taken second place around here lately."

He grinned sheepishly. "Sorry I'm late. We had a meeting after work to discuss our new insurance plan."

Tony talked for several minutes about the changes in policy.

". . . and with four children as dependents . . ."

"Five," I interrupted. "You're going to have five children."

"Five?" he repeated. "What do you mean?"

I waited for him to guess. He glanced at Melissa, then back to me.

"You mean . . . Melissa? We can keep her? Diane, are you serious?"

I nodded and told him about the call from Sarah.

"I can't believe it. Really? We can adopt her? I can't believe it," he repeated over and over.

Later, as I finished setting the table for supper, I heard him telling Melissa:

"Now you really are dad's girl. You're my number one daughter!"

The following evening, he returned from work with a small package in his hand. Inside was a miniature plate with gold lettering:

A Daughter Puts a Song in Your Heart.

11

An Answered Prayer

As the adoption process was set into motion, there were several telephone conversations with Barbara, the regional supervisor of the subsidized adoption program. I found her to be a warm, sympathetic, Christian woman. She did much to make the procedure less complicated.

The home study and visit by Dorothy, the assigned caseworker, determined that Melissa's medical needs (those relating to her birth defects) would be covered by funds from the adoption subsidy. This included any future need for adaptive equipment. Although the funds came through the state of Nebraska, Tony and I received it as a miracle of provision from the hand of God.

It was early in April when our attorney's secretary phoned to say the adoption petition was ready for our signatures. Tony signed the papers on the way to work and I dashed over later in the morning.

At the secretary's request, I took a seat and read

through the document to be certain the information was accurate. After several pages, I read the words for the first time: MELISSA LOVEY BAUMGARTNER. Over and over I read the name. Even if I'd wanted to I couldn't explain the emotions I felt.

Although the legal documents made no mention of it, Tony and I had agreed to an open adoption to allow continued contact with Melissa's biological family. It was uncertain what Sarah and I would eventually be comfortable with. She'd stated only a desire to phone and inquire about Melissa occasionally. I knew time would tell what was in God's plan but Tony and I hoped, despite impossible odds, that our relationship would continue to grow.

With Melissa's first birthday approaching, Sarah and Grandma Jean stopped by a few days early to leave their gifts. Sarah was wearing maternity clothes, just beginning to show the pregnancy with the new baby due in September. We talked briefly and I told them of another upcoming eye surgery. Once again, the pressure was elevated and Dr. Bush had arranged for a third operation.

The now familiar routine began in the admissions office where we waited, filled out our forms, and waited again. After what seemed an endless amount of time, we were sent to the fourth-floor pediatric clinic. There Melissa was examined by a pediatric intern. It always seemed ironic to me that one had to pass a physical examination before being admitted to the hospital for surgery.

When Melissa had been certified free from colds, measles, and all other contagious diseases, we were directed to the third floor and another wait in the eye clinic. We had managed to survive thus far and I knew a room would soon be assigned.

Our young surgical intern from the last hospitalization caught sight of us in the crowded waiting room.

"Why don't you just take Melissa on up to her room," he suggested. "I don't think we need to bother with the eye exam. I'm sure there's been no change."

I should have been pleased with the cut in red tape, but my response to the offer surprised me as much as it did the intern.

"No. I think you should check the pressure. We have been praying for Melissa and God may have healed her eyes."

The words came out of my mouth even before I'd thought about them. The intern said nothing, but closed Melissa's eyes and pressed his thumb cautiously against each lid, feeling for hardness.

"The eyes are soft! I think we'd better go into the examination room," he said in wide-eyed amazement.

I followed him down the hall, carrying Melissa into a small cubicle. The intern put drops into each eye. He placed the pressure reading instrument first on the left eye then on the right.

"I can't admit Melissa on these findings," he said, hurrying from the room to locate Dr. Bush.

A few moments later, the senior doctor bristled into the room.

"You can take Melissa to her room now."

"Aren't you going to take a pressure reading?" I asked.

"Oh, there's no need for that. It would be elevated as always."

"But I insist."

Realizing that I was determined, Dr. Bush closed

MELISSA

Melissa's eyes and pressed his thumbs against them in a hurried attempt to pacify me.

"Hmm . . . they do feel rather soft. Well, perhaps we should get a reading after all."

I waited on the edge of my chair for his findings.

"Well, I'll be . . ." he exclaimed. "This doesn't happen once in a thousand times. But then, what do I know? I'm only the doctor! The reading is normal. You can take Melissa home."

"Seems as if God gave his own birthday present to Melissa, doesn't it?" I smiled, thinking of the verse, "God hath chosen the foolish things of this world to confound the wise" (1 Cor. 1:20).

When Melissa and I arrived back home we found a package had arrived from my parents. I couldn't resist opening it, even though it was early. Melissa willingly modeled the spring dress and bonnet mother had chosen. Then I reached into the box and wound up the soft, yellow giraffe. Together we listened and I hummed along with the familiar tune from *Around the World in Eighty Days*. Tears rolled down my cheeks as I told her, "Yes, Melissa, I did know that someday I'd look at you and see the smile you're smiling now. And to me it's the most special gift of all."

While I prepared supper for the guests we'd invited to Melissa's party, the boys excitedly wrapped packages; a squeaky toy, a new rattle, a cuddly dolly we'd named Amy, and a tiny gold ring for her finger. Tony carried a long white box under his arm when he came home from work that evening. His extravagant love for Melissa was evident by the lavish gift he'd chosen; a dozen pink roses with a single red rose placed in the center.

He went to her and read the card: "Happy Birthday to the most beautiful girl in the whole wide world!"

Tenderly, he guided her small hands across each soft, dewy petal, then touched their cool dampness to her cheek.

For a split second, I looked at the roses and thought of their cost. Then I remembered a story from the Gospel of John where Mary used costly perfumed ointment to wash the feet of Jesus. When one of the disciples considered the act wasteful, Jesus reminded him:

"You will not always have me with you."

I thought of those words again as we lit the single birthday candle on Melissa's cake. The guests and family were seated and Melissa's roses stood in a tall vase in the center of the table. We sang the traditional "Happy Birthday," then followed with another favorite:

"A happy birthday to you, a happy birthday to you,
May you feel Jesus near, every day of the year.
A happy birthday to you, a happy birthday to you,
May God bless you and keep you this whole year
     through!"

With Shannon's help Melissa's birthday candle was blown out and her finger dipped into the chocolate frosting. When the gifts had been opened and the cake and ice cream finished, Melissa drank a warm bottle and drifted off to sleep in Rob's arms. Later, as I tucked her into bed and snuggled Amy close in her arms, I whispered softly into her ear, "Yes, Melissa. May God keep you this whole year through."

It had been a special day. Now, with great anticipation, Tony and I looked forward to the next celebration— Melissa's dedication to the Lord.

A few weeks later we joined the other parents in the

front row of the sanctuary. Together, we had come with our children, just as Samuel's parents did in the Old Testament, taking him to the temple at Shiloh. The words from First Samuel seemed to be my own: "For this child I prayed; and the Lord has given me the petition I made to Him. Therefore, I have lent him to the Lord; as long as he lives, he is lent to the Lord" (1:27, 28).

Following an opening prayer and worship in song, Pastor Murdoch called for the parents to come forward with their children. We formed a semicircle in the front of the church.

"Sometimes," pastor began, "we have fidgety children like these two little boys, and sometimes we have quiet babies like Melissa. But the Lord doesn't mind the chatter and the wiggliness. He sees the hearts of the parents who have come before him. . . ."

One by one, pastor took each child into his arms as he prayed and moved down the long row. At last, it was Melissa's turn.

"Melissa Lovey . . . soon to be the adopted daughter of Tony and Diane." We bowed our heads as pastor placed his hands tenderly on Melissa's head and prayed:

"Melissa, may the Lord bless you and keep you. The Lord cause his face to shine upon you and be gracious unto you. The Lord lift up his countenance upon you and give you grace.

"May you be God's little evangelist. May God use your life as a door through which your parents might share the love of God with others. Though you may never speak a single word, Melissa, may others come to know Christ because of the influence of your life. . . . We dedicate you now to the Lord."

Later that week, as I wrote the adoption announcement, I read the words, "The handiwork of God—a new hand in ours." It reminded me of Ephesians 2:10: "For we are God's handiwork, created in Christ Jesus to devote ourselves to the good deeds for which God has designed us" (NEB).

Because of her birth defects, perhaps not many would have considered Melissa to be God's handiwork. But Tony and I had often talked of the way our love for Melissa was a constant reminder of the way in which God loved us. "For a long time, although God continually showed us his love, we didn't respond to it," Tony said. "We gave Melissa love and affection for months before we were certain she was aware of our love.

"When we received Christ as Lord and Savior we had nothing to offer him but ourselves and our need. In a similar way, Melissa came to us offering us nothing—not even a promising future. She had only a need to be loved and accepted just as she was.

"To adopt Melissa was to give her no less than what God had given us—the free gift of love, a family to belong to, and unconditional acceptance."

12

Miraculously, Our Own

The cool, early morning breeze drifted across my face. Sleepily, I opened my eyes and looked at Melissa in her crib. She was awake, lying quietly on her side waiting for signs of movement from me. In her arm, she held Amy cuddled close against her tummy.

"Good morning, 'Liss," I whispered, kissing her cheek. "Did you have a nice sleep, sweetheart? Did you know today is a special day for mommy and daddy?"

Tony rolled over, yawned and stretched. "Is my girl awake?" he asked. "Bring her here so daddy can kiss her."

I took Melissa's dolly, and the blankets and pillows that positioned her during the night, and placed them at the foot of the crib. Gently, I snuggled her against my neck and we slipped back into bed.

For a long while, I held Tony's hand and looked at the

baby lying between us. It was a moment to cherish. A moment of tenderness to remember.

Special times always seem to be fleeting. Ours was blasted away by an explosion of awakening teenagers. We heard bedroom doors slamming. Soon the shower was running. Then came a cry of, "Mom! Where's my brown shirt?" Like a whoosh of dandelion fluff the moment was gone.

"Sounds as if our boys are up," Tony said.

He left to put the coffee on while I answered the ringing telephone. It was Mr. Ryan, our attorney.

"I have to be in another courtroom at nine o'clock, Diane. No need for you folks to wait the extra hour, so I'll meet you around ten."

Hurray, I almost shouted, *time for me to get ready at a decent pace. Maybe even time for breakfast.*

"Tony," I called. "Mr. Ryan phoned and we have another hour. How about going out to eat?"

"Good idea," he answered.

When Melissa had been fed, bathed, and drenched in sweet-smelling baby lotion, I dressed her in red leotards and tiny patent-leather shoes. The navy-blue dress magnified the blue of her eyes. White, lacy ruffles around her neck and bottom emphasized "girl." The crowning touch was a white bow in the Kewpie-doll curl on the top of her head.

"Are you ready, family?" I called to Tony and the boys. The pageantry began as they stood for Melissa's grand entrance. Like debutantes at a coming-out party, we descended the staircase; slowly, grandly, royally.

Our five male admirers applauded and laughed with delight. They were most appreciative of the dramatics. Cries and giggles of "Isn't she sweet?" and "Oh, mom, she looks so cute!" rose to greet us.

When we reached the final step, I paused to make an announcement:

"Gentlemen, may I present to you your soon-to-be sister and daughter!"

Bouquets of hugs and kisses were showered on us. But, alas, our moment of sweet glory was soon passed and the praise turned to cries of: "Let's go eat, I'm hungry" and "Me, too, I'm starved."

"Typical," I whispered in Melissa's ear.

Before long, our exuberant family descended on the pancake house. After the waitress had taken our orders, we joined hands, forming a circle around the table as we prayed.

"Thank you, Lord, for this special day; the day Melissa becomes our child. We remember with gratefulness the happy days on which each of our boys were born—the gift they were to us then and the joy they are to us now.

"Bless this food now. Let it nourish our bodies. Amen."

As we ate, the boys besieged us with questions:

"Will we go before the judge, too?"

"Where will we sit?"

"Will Melissa's name be the same as ours now?"

"Will she really be ours, so we can do anything we want with her, like move or something?"

Tony patiently answered questions. I couldn't help noting how different they were from the ones asked only a few months ago:

"What will we do if something happened to Melissa?"

"I don't know if we should adopt her. What if she should die?"

"What about when we go on vacation? Will we take her along? Because I don't think we should."

Somehow, God had supplied the answers to all those questions. And in the process, we had learned a precious truth: *you don't have to be afraid to love someone you can't keep forever.*

"Let's wash up and be on our way," Tony said, noting the time. Ten minutes later we were in front of the old stone courthouse. Tony let Melissa and me out of the car while he and the boys found a parking spot.

We waited on a bench near a spraying fountain of water. I watched the people rushing by. What are they doing today, I wondered. Shopping? Running errands?

Tony and the boys rounded the corner and together we climbed the long marble steps into the courthouse and took the elevator to the third floor.

Mr. Ryan waved as we approached. "Go right in and have a seat, folks. I'll be with you in a minute."

Inside the small courtroom, we took our places in the observer's gallery. My eyes drank in the scene. High, ornate ceilings, the witness stand, oak benches; it could have been the setting for an old western movie. Most of the courtrooms had recently been renovated, but I liked the character of this old room.

Our attorney joined us and Tony introduced him to Melissa and the boys. Then Judge Wilson, still dressed in street clothes, came out of his chambers and shook hands with all of us. He was a small man, with dark-rimmed glasses and slightly graying hair. I especially liked his smile. When the judge returned to his chambers, Mr. Ryan asked us to look over the adoption decree once again to recheck its accuracy.

Soon a tall, thin bailiff took his position near the witness stand and banged his gavel.

"Will all please rise."

We rose to our feet as the black-robed judge moved to his place behind the high bench. Mr. Ryan was the first to speak.

"Your Honor, with your permission may we have the Baumgartner family approach the bench at this time?"

The judge nodded his head in approval.

We weren't expecting this! We'd been told only Tony and I would approach the bench. It was a special blessing to have the boys included. Together we formed a line in front of Judge Wilson. The boys beamed as the attorney continued:

"Your Honor, I present the Baumgartner family, here today for the purpose of the adoption of Melissa."

Mr. Ryan then handed the documents to the judge. For several minutes he examined the papers, then peered over the top of his glasses.

"How old is Melissa?" he asked.

"Just over one year, your honor," I replied.

"Would each of you please state your name for the record."

The boys elbowed each other. They even got to speak! Their chests seemed to puff with pride as they gave their names.

Judge Wilson continued. "Raise your right hands, please," he said, looking at Tony and me.

"Do you freely and willingly adopt this child? And do you promise to give her all the rights and privileges afforded your natural children?"

"I do," we replied, as I held Melissa between us.

Then addressing the boys with just a hint of a smile and a mischievous twinkle in his eyes, Judge Wilson instructed them to raise their right hands. Surprise was written across their faces. This was just too much! They were going to be sworn in also.

"Repeat after me," he told them. "I do solemnly promise to change diapers, to baby-sit, to . . ."

Stunned, the boys were speechless for several seconds.

MELISSA

Their mouths dropped open. But in a flash, the swearing-in hands were down and voices returned with, "Oh, no. Not me!"

We roared with laughter at the great joke the judge had played on the boys. When we'd regained our composure, Judge Wilson spoke the words we had been waiting to hear.

"Congratulations, Melissa is now your daughter."

Tony leaned over and kissed first Melissa, then me. There were tears in our eyes. The boys hugged Melissa and congratulated us.

We left the courtroom and passed a bulletin board in the hall. A lovely poster caught my attention. A mother was holding her little girl in her arms as they sat in a meadow. I stopped to read the words:

Love for One More

The Answer
To an adopted child

Not flesh of my flesh
Nor bone of my bone,
but still miraculously
my own.
Never forget
for a single minute
you didn't grow
under my heart . . .
but in it!

Anonymous

Epilogue

*"And you will know the truth, and
the truth will set you free."*
                John 8:32

As a family, we had talked often of the day when Melissa
would have a whole, well, new body in heaven. With great
pleasure we thought of her walking and running. And we
smiled when we considered what her first words might
be—when she beheld Jesus through eyes no longer blind.
No, there was no question about the things that would
happen for Melissa *after* death. We knew her spirit would
immediately go to be with God. It was only the events
which would occur at the *time* of death which filled us
with uncertainty.

Careful plans had been made for Melissa's education
and medical needs and, as adoption day approached, it
seemed increasingly irresponsible to delay preparation
for her death until it became a painful, present reality.
There was time, now. Time to pray and seek God's direction without the pressure of immediate need.

Still, the decision to face my own fears regarding

MELISSA

Melissa's death came with many struggles. It seemed almost unthinkable to scar happy days—days when Melissa was well and progressing—with discussions of funeral arrangements. How could one prepare for adoption and death simultaneously? *Adoption* spoke of permanancy and planning. Death was the reminder that all our days on earth are impermanent and fleeting.

Perhaps it would not come next week, next month, or even next year, but there would be a day when God would call Melissa home to heaven. And I wanted to be ready, with no regrets later of, "Why didn't we . . ." and "I wish we had . . ."

Tony and I made arrangements to visit several nearby mortuaries, wondering how we would know which would be the right choice for us.

The confirmation we had hoped for came when we met Dick Wessling, a tall, husky mortician in his late thirties. For some time we talked with him about the steps that would occur from the time of death until burial. It was Dick's response which gave us the indication that, of all the funeral homes in our city, being led to this one was no mere coincidence. This mortician had a special love for the handicapped! Dick and his wife, Mary Ann, were the parents of three learning-disabled children. In a way that others could not, Dick understood about our love for Melissa. We knew that when the time came, he would care for Melissa's body in death even as we now cared for it in life.

That afternoon as we left the mortuary we couldn't know that the Wessling family and ours would one day become dear friends. We only knew that the fear and uncertainty were gone because of a loving God—a God who cared for even the smallest concerns of the human heart. With a new sense of expectancy, we looked forward now to the coming days with Melissa as a celebration of life itself.

One of the loveliest, happiest parts of that celebration was discovered in God's unique plan for the open-adoption agreement with Sarah and David. It was David who telephoned to share the joyful news of the arrival of their new baby, a healthy second son.

And over a period of months, my friendship with Sarah grew like a slowly opening rose; each tightly closed petal unfolded gradually. In the early days after Melissa's adoption, Sarah and I were hesitant about phoning and visiting one another, each uncertain of the other's desires. But in time, those doubts were replaced with the confidence of an old and trusted friendship. As Sarah once expressed it, "God has used Melissa as a bridge, bringing our lives together."

At first our conversations were mostly about Melissa, but as time passed we frequently talked about the things of God. Sarah was healing. And as her pain subsided she found answers to the questions asked long ago at the hospital window.

After Sarah committed her life to the Lord, she began to be not only my friend, but my sister in the Lord!

It was some weeks before Sarah realized what her new commitment to Christ would mean eternally, for her and Melissa. She was excited with her new discovery when she phoned one Sunday evening:

"Just think! I *will* be with Melissa again someday. We'll know one another. The things that have happened here are only for a time, but heaven is *forever*. And if it hadn't been for Melissa, maybe I wouldn't have found Jesus at all!"

For two years, nine months, and nineteen days, it was our marvelous privilege to share Melissa's life. On Feb-

MELISSA

ruary 10th, 1980, six months after Sarah received Jesus as her Savior, Melissa received the new spiritual body we had talked of so often. And three weeks later, to the very hour, Ann, the social worker who brought Melissa into our lives, left my side at church to walk forward and receive Christ.

Melissa
Your smile was not a smile,
but a miracle.
Your life was not a tragedy,
but a gift . . .
Opening the hearts of those
With arms long enough to reach
into your near nonexistence
and draw you to light.
Your eyes held a private world
only those with love could see.
Your stillness was a handicap
for others to overcome.
Your silence spoke gentle words,
teaching others of faith, hope,
and beauty.
Your short life gave to those around you
more than they could give to themselves.
Your legacy was love . . .
left in the hearts of others.
JILL MORSE